THE NEW COOKBOOK FOR ATHLETES

100 DELICIOUS RECIPES TO HELP YOU BUILD MUSCLE

FRED SHORTS

All rights reserved.

Disclaimer

The information contained in this eBook is meant to serve as a comprehensive collection of strategies that the author of this eBook has done research about. Summaries, strategies, tips, and tricks are only recommended by the author, and reading this eBook will not guarantee that one's results will exactly mirror the author's results. The author of the eBook has made all reasonable efforts to provide current and accurate information for the readers of the eBook. The author and its associates will not be held liable for any unintentional error or omissions that may be found. The material in the eBook may include information from third parties. Third-party materials comprise opinions expressed by their owners. As such, the author of the eBook does not assume responsibility or liability for any third-party material or opinions. Whether because of the progression of the internet, or the unforeseen changes in company policy and editorial submission guidelines, what is stated as fact at the time of this writing may become outdated or inapplicable later.

The eBook is copyright © 2022 with all rights reserved. It is illegal to redistribute, copy, or create derivative work from this eBook in whole or in part. No parts of this report may be reproduced or retransmitted in any reproduced or retransmitted in any forms whatsoever without the writing expressed and signed permission from the author.

TABLE OF CONTENTS

TABLE OF CONTENTS...3
INTRODUCTION...7
    1. PROTEIN MEATBALLS...9
    2. TURKEY, APPLE AND SAGE MEATBALLS.......................................11
    3. ASIAN MEATBALLS WITH HOISIN APPLE GLAZE..........................14
    4. ROASTED ACORN SQUASH WITH CHICKEN MEATBALLS.............18
    5. SUPERFOOD OVERNIGHT OATS..22
    6. SPICY CHICKEN WITH COUSCOUS...24
    7. SPEEDY HARISSA CHICKEN AND TABBOULEH...............................27
    8. ONE-TRAY CASHEW CHICKEN..30
    9. LOAF TIN LASAGNE..33
    10. HARISSA CHICKEN AND MOROCCAN COUSCOUS........................36
    11. BUFFALO CHICKEN PASTA SALAD..39
    12. CHICKEN, SWEET POTATO AND GREENS.....................................42
    13. ASIAN PEANUT BUTTER SESAME CHICKEN..................................45
    14. BARBECUE CHICKEN AND RICE..48
    15. LOW-CAL LIME AND CHILLI TURKEY BURGERS............................51
    16. MALAYSIAN CHICKEN SATAY...53
    17. CHICKEN TIKKA MASALA..57
    18. ONE-POT COCONUT CHICKEN AND RICE MEAL PREP..................60
    19. BBQ PULLED CHICKEN MAC N CHEESE.......................................64
    20. PEANUT BUTTER CHICKEN CURRY...68
    21. FAJITA PASTA BAKE...71
    22. CREAMY LEMON AND THYME CHICKEN......................................74
    23. CHICKEN AND CHORIZO PAELLA...77
    24. EASY PROTEIN BOWL MEAL PREP..80
    25. SEARED TUNA STEAK AND SWEET POTATO WEDGES.................84
    26. QUICK SPICY CAJUN SALMON AND GARLICKY VEG....................88
    27. TUNA PASTA SALAD..91
    28. SALMON POKE BOWL..94

29. HIGH-PROTEIN KEDGEREE...97
30. SPICED LAMB WITH FETA BULGUR...100
31. LEAN, CREAMY SAUSAGE PASTA..103
32. SWEET POTATO AND CHORIZO HASH...106
33. TERIYAKI BEEF ZOODLES..109
34. BAKED FETA COUSCOUS...112
35. ONE-POT LENTIL DAHL...115
36. SWEET PAPRIKA VEGAN BOWL AND CHOCOLATE PROTEIN BALLS.......119
37. ULTIMATE 15-MINUTE VEGAN FAJITAS...123
38. CRISPY TOFU AND TERIYAKI NOODLES..126
39. VEGAN LENTIL BOLOGNESE..130
40. BREAKFAST BURRITOS FOR ALL WEEK LONG...................................133
41. BURRITO JARS..137
42. ULTIMATE HIGH-PROTEIN STUFFED PEPPERS 4 WAYS......................140
43. ITALIAN CHICKEN MEATBALLS WITH SPAGHETTI..............................142
44. MEDITERRANEAN TURKEY MEATBALLS WITH TZATZIKI....................146
45. VEGGIE AND BEEF MEATBALLS MARINARA......................................150
46. HONEY BARBECUE CHICKEN MEATBALLS..153
47. TURKEY SWEET POTATO MEATBALLS..156
48. EASY MEXICAN CHICKPEA SALAD..158
49. TOFU AND SPINACH CANNELLONI...161
50. COCONUT CURRY LENTIL SOUP...164
51. INDIAN CURRY QUINOA...167
52. GRILLED VEGETABLES ON WHITE BEAN MASH.................................170
53. OVEN ROASTED SEITAN...173
54. CHICKPEA TOFU...176
55. BRAISED TOFU...179
56. SPICY PEANUT BUTTER TEMPEH..182
57. SMOKY CHICKPEA TUNA SALAD..185
58. THAI QUINOA SALAD...188
59. TURKISH BEAN SALAD...191
60. VEGETABLE AND QUINOA BOWLS...194
61. ALMOND BUTTER TOFU STIR-FRY...197
62. QUINOA CHICKPEA BUDDHA BOWL..200
63. SEITAN PARMESAN..203
64. RED LENTIL PATTIES..206

65. ARUGULA PESTO AND ZUCCHINI..209
66. VEGETARIAN CASSEROLE..212
67. ROASTED BRUSSELS SPROUTS...215
68. AVOCADO CHICKPEA SANDWICH...217
69. SKILLET QUINOA..219
70. STICKY TOFU WITH NOODLES..222
71. VEGAN BBQ TERIYAKI TOFU...225
72. SPROUTS WITH GREEN BEANS..228
73. CRUSTED TOFU WITH RADISH...230
74. LENTIL LASAGNA...233
75. LENTIL MEATBALLS...236
76. HAZELNUT-CRUSTED PORK MEDALLIONS..239
77. PORK CHOPS WITH RELISH..242
78. PORK WITH SPAGHETTI SQUASH..245
79. SPICY QUINOA FALAFEL..248
80. BUTTERNUT SQUASH GALETTE...251
81. QUINOA WITH CURRY PASTE...254
82. BAKED SMOKY CARROT BACON..257
83. SALMON OVER SPAGHETTI SQUASH..259
84. POACHED SALMON ON LEEKS...262
85. GRILLED SWORDFISH WITH SALSA...264
86. TUNA STEAKS WITH MAYO..266
87. SQUASHED WINTER SQUASH..268
88. SKEWERED SCALLOPS PROSCIUTTO...270
89. SEITAN AND BLACK BEAN..273
90. CURRIED TOFU COVERS...276
91. THAI SALAD WITH TEMPEH...279
92. PUFFED QUINOA BAR...281
93. CHOCOLATE CHUNK COOKIES..283
94. SHELLED EDAMAME DIP..286
95. MATCHA CASHEW CUPS..288
96. CHICKPEA CHOCO SLICES...290
97. SWEET GREEN COOKIES...292
98. BANANA BARS...294
99. PROTEIN DONUTS...297
100. HONEY-SESAME TOFU..300

CONCLUSION..303

INTRODUCTION

Nobody pays quite as much attention to what they eat as a bodybuilder. The calories have to be right and macros have to be balanced, and we can't forget about the micros, either.

Then there are the various diet philosophies that contend for the pole position — intermittent fasting, carbohydrate cycling, ketogenic, and flexible dieting, to name a few. Well, regardless of your preferences, these bodybuilding recipes will have you covered.

You'll find a little bit of everything here to help make your meal prepping a success, from high-calorie and high-carb to low-carbohydrate and low-carbohydrate, fast and easy to more involved (and rewarding!). Oh and there's plenty of protein too, of course!

Bodybuilding is a delicate balance between building muscle and burning fat. You need adequate calories to increase muscle mass, but you also need a caloric deficit to burn off stored fat. It sounds impossible, but it isn't. The secret? Basic math. Or, as it's referred to in the fitness world: the Energy Balance Equation. Simply put, the more muscle mass you have, and the more active you are, the more you need to eat. That's because the more lean muscle mass you have, the more energy (thanks, food!) it takes to move that muscle around. Anything from basic functions like breathing, digestion, and your heart beating, to walking around and carrying the laundry up the stairs, or more deliberate exercise like running or pushing serious weight in the gym—your body needs energy, and if you're doing all these tasks with more lean muscle, you need more fuel.

Before you go running to the fridge, let's look at the other end of the spectrum. When we eat more calories than our body uses, all those extra calories are stored as fat. This is the reason why many people who gorge to get strong, never actually become lean and shredded. They may indeed get stronger, but getting lean means cutting out extra calories. There are still other factors to consider, like poor food quality, lack of nutrient timing, and improper ratios of macronutrients. All calories are, of course, not created equal. We want to fuel our body with the best building blocks, at the right time to power our workout, improve our performance, grow more muscle, and get rid of extra body fat.

1. **Protein Meatballs**

Serves: 12

Ingredients:

- 0.8 - 1 lb lean ground beef (95% lean meat/5% fat)
- 1 small yellow onion, grated
- ¼ cup fresh parsley, minced
- 1 egg
- ⅓ cup dry bread crumbs
- 1 teaspoon salt and ½ teaspoon pepper

Directions:

a) Preheat oven to 425 degrees.

b) Line a rimmed baking sheet with parchment paper.

c) Combine all **Ingredients** in to a mixing bowl. Using your hands, gently combine **Ingredients** until well incorporated.

d) Form meat in to balls, 1-inch in diameter by gently rolling between your hands. Place on baking sheet, leaving at least 1-inch between each one.

e) Bake for 12 minutes. Remove from oven and serve or add to marinara.

2. Turkey, Apple and Sage Meatballs

Serves: 20

Ingredients:

- 1½-2 lbs ground turkey
- 1 large apple, grated (about 1 cup, packed; peel if you prefer, but I didn't)
- ½ cup finely chopped sweet onion
- 2 large eggs, beaten
- 2 tablespoons coconut flour
- 2 lightly-packed tablespoons chopped fresh sage leaves
- ½ teaspoon nutmeg
- Generous pinch of salt
- ½ teaspoon ground black pepper

Directions:

a) In a large mixing bowl, stir together the turkey, apple, onion, eggs, and coconut flour until combined. Then stir in the sage, nutmeg, salt and pepper until the flavors are evenly distributed.

b) Scoop into 3 tablespoon balls and roll between your palms to smooth them out.

c) Preheat the oven to 350 and preheat a couple of tablespoons of oil in an oven-safe skillet. Sauté the meatballs, at least an inch apart, until the bottom is dark brown and crispy (about 3-5 minutes) and then flip and do the same on the other side.

d) Transfer the pan into the preheated oven and bake for 9-12 minutes until cooked through (no pink remains in the center). Mine were perfect at 10 minutes.

e) Store cooked or uncooked meatballs in an airtight container in the fridge for up to 3 days, or in the freezer for up to 3 months.

3. Asian Meatballs with Hoisin Apple Glaze

Serves: 24

Ingredients:

For the meatballs

- ½ lb cremini mushrooms, roughly chopped (stems removed)
- 1 cup All-Bran Original cereal
- 1 lb extra lean ground turkey
- 1 egg
- 1 clove of garlic, finely minced
- ½ teaspoon toasted sesame oil
- 1 teaspoon reduced sodium soy sauce
- 2 tablespoons cilantro, finely chopped
- 2 tablespoons green onions, finely chopped
- ¼ teaspoon salt
- ¼ teaspoon pepper

For the sauce and garnish

- ¼ cup hoisin sauce
- ¼ cup rice wine vinegar

- 1 cup unsweetened apple sauce
- 2 tablespoons apple butter
- 1 tablespoon reduced sodium soy sauce
- 1 teaspoon sesame oil

Optional garnishes

- Peanuts, crushed
- Green onions, thinly sliced
- Sesame seeds

Directions:

For the meatballs:

a) Preheat oven to 400 F and line a large baking sheet with parchment paper or a silpat.

b) Using a food processor, pulse the mushrooms until they reach a ground meat-like consistency. Transfer to a bowl.

c) Add the All-Bran to the food processor and process until it reaches a powder. Add to the bowl.

d) Mix in the turkey, egg, garlic, toasted sesame oil, soy sauce, cilantro, green onions, salt and pepper. Roll into 24 balls and place on the baking sheet.

e) Bake for 15-18 minutes, or until golden brown on the outside, and fully cooked on the inside.

For the sauce and garnish:

f) In a large sauce pan, combine the hoisin sauce, vinegar, apple sauce, apple butter, soy sauce and sesame oil and simmer over medium low heat until fully combined and thick.

To assemble:

g) Once the meatballs are cooked, add them to the pan with the sauce and toss until well coated.

h) Garnish with crushed peanuts, sesame seeds and sliced green onion, if desired.

4. Roasted Acorn Squash with Chicken Meatballs

Serves: 4

Ingredients:

- 2 acorn squash
- 1 tablespoon olive oil
- Sea salt and fresh ground pepper
- 3 cloves garlic, minced
- 3 scallions, coarsely chopped
- 1 cup cilantro leaves (stems removed)
- 1 lb. extra lean ground chicken
- 2 teaspoons ground cumin
- ¼ cup panko
- ¼ to ½ cup Hatch green chile, chopped
- 2 tablespoons pine nuts
- ¼ cup Cotija cheese – crumbled (optional)
- 1 avocado, skin and pit removed
- 2 tablespoons plain yogurt
- 1 tablespoon olive oil mayonnaise

- Buttermilk to thin if necessary
- Additional cilantro to garnish

Directions:

a) Preheat oven to 400 degrees (375 degrees in convection oven). Carefully slice both ends of your squash. Slice the remaining piece into rounds from 1½ to 3-inches – that may be 2 or 3 pieces. Place on a baking sheet, brush with olive oil, and season with salt and pepper. Place in the center of your preheated oven for 15 to 20 minutes while you make the filling.

b) To the bowl of a food processor, add the garlic, scallions, and cilantro. Pulse a few times until finely chopped but not pureed.

c) Add the cilantro mixture to a large mixing bowl with the ground chicken. Add the cumin and panko. Mix well. Hands work best! Fold in the green chile, pine nuts, and cotija if using. Don't overmix, but do try to incorporate throughout the chicken mixture. Form into 4-5 balls depending on number of acorn squash slices and your preferences.

d) Remove squash from the oven. Place a meatball into the center of each slice. Return to the oven for about 25 additional minutes. The time depends on the size of your meatballs. If you insert a fork into the meatball, it should be fairly firm, and the squash should be quite tender.

e) While the meatballs and squash are cooking, combine the avocado, yogurt, mayonnaise, salt and pepper in a blender or food processor. Process until smooth. Check seasoning. Add buttermilk to desired consistency. I like it a little looser than mayonnaise—thick, not runny!

f) When ready to serve, place a dollop of the avocado crema on each serving, and garnish with cilantro. Enjoy!

5. Superfood Overnight Oats

Serves: 1

Ingredients

- 75g dairy-free yoghurt
- 50g Instant Oats
- 125ml almond milk
- 1 Tablespoon Almond Butter
- 1 teaspoon cinnamon
- Pinch salt

Directions

a) Mix all **Ingredients** in a jar or bowl and stir well.

b) Cover and refrigerate for at least 4 hours or overnight, then enjoy your deliciously plump and creamy overnight oats!

6. Spicy Chicken With Couscous

Servings 4

Ingredients

- 1 Tablespoon curry paste
- 1 Tablespoon mango chutney
- 1/2 teaspoon turmeric
- 1 serving salt (to taste)
- 50 ml olive oil
- 4 chicken breasts
- 300 g couscous
- 350 ml vegetable stock
- Optional extras:
- Pomegranate seeds
- Coriander

Directions

a) To make a marinade for your chicken, add the curry paste, chutney, turmeric, salt and olive oil to a bowl and mix it well.

b) Cut each chicken breast in half before adding to the marinade. Stir well until all of the chicken is covered.

c) Leave the chicken aside for at least 20 minutes — ideally in the fridge overnight.

d) Heat a grill pan over medium heat and lay out your chicken pieces. Grill the chicken pieces for 5-6 minutes on each side, or until golden and slightly charred.

e) Meanwhile, place the couscous in a big bowl and carefully pour in the boiling vegetable stock. Cover the bowl with a lid and leave to the couscous to soak for around 5 minutes.

f) Fluff your couscous with a fork and add any extras you want. Pomegranate seeds are great for a colour and flavour.

g) Divide your couscous into 4 containers before topping with two pieces of marinated chicken. Finish the dish with a sprinkle of coriander.

7. Speedy Harissa Chicken and Tabbouleh

Makes: 4 meals

Ingredients

- 50 g harissa paste
- 1 teaspoon extra virgin olive oil
- 1 pinch seal salt
- 3 x chicken breast (try skin-on for extra flavour)
- 180 g bulgar wheat or couscous (dry weight)
- 40 g parsley (stems and leaves)
- 20 g mint leaves
- 6-8 x spring onions
- 1/2 a cucumber
- 4 x tomatoes
- 6 Tablespoon Greek yoghurt
- 1/2 a lemon (juice and zest)
- 1 clove of garlic (minced)
- 1 pinch of sea salt
- 1 handful of pomegranate seeds (optional)

Directions

a) For the chicken: Preheat the oven to 190°C. In a small bowl, mix the harissa paste, olive oil, and a pinch of salt.

b) Score the tops of the chicken breasts with a sharp knife, then rub the harissa mixture over the chicken breasts and into the score lines.

c) Whilst waiting, make the tabbouleh. Cook bulgar wheat or couscous according to the directions on the back of the pack. Once cooked, drain, pour into a large mixing bowl and separate the grains with a fork. Allow to cool.

d) Finely chop the parsley, mint leaves, spring onions, cucumber and

e) For the dressing: Simply combine the Greek yoghurt, lemon juice and zest, minced garlic, and sea salt in a bowl.

f) Once all components are ready, divide amongst three Tupperware containers. Allow to cool, then refrigerate and store for up to 3 days.

8. One-Tray Cashew Chicken

Makes: 4 meals

Ingredients

- 3 Tablespoon Cashew Butter
- 2 Tablespoon soy sauce
- 2 Tablespoon Maple or Agave Syrup
- 2 cloves garlic
- 1 teaspoon Chinese five spice
- 4 chicken breasts (diced)
- 1 head broccoli (cut into florets)
- 40g cashew nuts
- 2 red chillies (diced)
- Handful fresh coriander
- 300g basmati rice (cooked)

Directions

a) Preheat oven to 200°C or 180°C for fan-assisted. In a large bowl, whisk together cashew butter, soy sauce, maple syrup, garlic and five spice.

b) Add the diced chicken and broccoli florets to the bowl and coat well.

c) Pour the contents of the bowl into a deep baking tray and bake for 20 minutes.

d) Meanwhile, toast your cashew nuts. Heat a frying pan on a high heat, add the cashews and don't move them until they begin to brown and pop a little. Toss and allow to brown on the other side.

e) Once the cashew chicken and broccoli are baked, stir through the cashew nuts and chillies, divide and place into Tupperware boxes with the cooked basmati rice. Sprinkle a little chopped coriander over each and refrigerate. Easy!

9. Loaf Tin Lasagne

Makes: 4 portions

Ingredients

- 1 teaspoon Coconut Oil
- 1 white onion, coarsely chopped
- 2 cloves garlic, finely chopped
- 1 Tablespoon dried oregano
- 350g turkey mince
- 600g chopped tomatoes or tomato passata
- 300g lasagne sheets
- 1 courgette
- 1 teaspoon sea salt and black pepper
- 400g cottage cheese
- 3 egg whites
- 100g low-fat cheese (grated)

Directions

a) First, make your turkey ragu. Add the coconut oil to a pan on a medium to high heat. Add the onion and sauté for 3-4 minutes, then add the garlic and sauté for a further 2 minutes (if you're using the powdered versions, add them after the next step).

b) Next, add the turkey mince and break it up a little using a spatula, then allow it to brown for 3-4 minutes, stirring occasionally. Stir in the oregano, $\frac{1}{2}$ teaspoon salt and pepper and the tomatoes and simmer on a low heat for 10 minutes.

c) While you're waiting, whisk cottage cheese and egg whites together in a bowl using a fork with the remaining salt and pepper. Set aside. Preheat the oven at 200°C or 180°C for fan-assisted.

d) Now prepare your courgette and lasagne sheets. Use a vegetable peeler to slice the courgette lengthways to get long slices. Wash the lasagne sheets under cold water in a colander.

e) Once the turkey ragu is ready, it's time to make up the lasagne. Start with a layer of courgette sheets for easy removal once cooked. Then alternate between the ragu, cheese sauce, lasagne sheets, and courgette. Finish with a layer of lasagne, then cheese sauce, then sprinkle with low-fat cheese.

f) Bake for 15 minutes with foil on, then remove the foil, turn the heat up by 20°C and bake for a further 20 minutes. Once cooked, divide into four meal prep containers, serve with your favourite salad or vegetables and store in the fridge for up to three days.

10. Harissa Chicken and Moroccan Couscous

Serves 4

Ingredients

- 500 g boneless, skinless chicken thighs
- 1 Tablespoon extra virgin olive oil
- 2 Tablespoon harissa paste
- ½ lemon (juiced)
- 1 onion (finely chopped)
- 3 garlic cloves (crushed)
- 2 Tablespoon coconut oil
- 1 teaspoon cumin
- 1 teaspoon smoked paprika
- 350 g couscous
- 1 vegetable stock cube
- 1 litre boiled water
- 1 bunch fresh parsley (finely chopped)
- 1 teaspoon chilli flakes
- 40 g pine nuts
- 50 g raisins

Directions

a) First, add the olive oil, harissa paste, salt, pepper, and lemon juice to your chicken thighs and massage the paste into them. Once coated, set aside and leave to marinade.

b) Meanwhile, chop the onion and garlic, then heat a tablespoon of coconut oil in a non-stick pan. Add the onion and cook for 5 minutes until soft.

c) Add the garlic to pan and cook for 2 minutes before adding the cumin and smoked paprika. Stir spices into onion and garlic, then stir in the dry couscous.

d) Mix your veg stock and boiling water together, then add to the pan. Stir everything until combined and leave couscous to soak up liquid.

e) Meanwhile, heat the remaining tablespoon of coconut oil in a cast iron pan or griddle on high heat. Add the harissa chicken thighs and cook for 4-5 minutes on each side, before removing from pan and setting aside.

f) Once couscous has soaked up veg stock and doubled in size, transfer to large bowl and add the raisins, pine nuts, parsley, juice of $\frac{1}{2}$ a lemon, salt, pepper, and chilli flakes.

g) Add a bed of couscous to each of your meal prep containers and top with the sliced harissa chicken.

11. Buffalo Chicken Pasta Salad

Makes: 3 meals

Ingredients

For the pasta:

- 160g cooked pasta
- 3 breasts cooked chicken
- 2 stalks celery
- Handful cherry tomatoes
- 1 yellow pepper
- 2 Tablespoon reduced-fat ranch dressing
- Large handful mixed leaves

For the buffalo sauce:

- 175ml peri-peri sauce
- ½ teaspoon garlic powder
- 4 Tablespoon reduced-fat butter or margarine
- Pinch salt

Directions

a) Place a saucepan over a medium heat and add the peri-peri sauce and garlic powder. Cook for 2 minutes, then add butter and salt and cook for a further 5 minutes, stirring occasionally. Remove from the heat and allow to cool for a few minutes.

b) Chop celery, tomatoes and pepper into bite-size pieces, and then shred the chicken using two forks. Place into a large mixing bowl with the cooked pasta.

c) Pour over buffalo sauce and toss it through the pasta salad. Divide amongst 3 meal-prep containers and drizzle a little ranch dressing over each, and serve with a handful of mixed leaves or your favourite side salad. Refrigerate for up to 3 days and enjoy hot or cold.

12. Chicken, Sweet Potato and Greens

Ingredients

- 2 Tablespoon Coconut Oil
- 4 x 130g chicken breast
- 350g sweet potato
- 1/2 teaspoon sea salt
- 1/2 teaspoon black pepper
- 1/2 teaspoon paprika
- 1 bag fresh spinach
- 350g green beans (trimmed)
- Sprinkle of chosen spices

Directions

a) Preheat the oven to 180°C.

b) Firstly, start by cutting your sweet potatoes into wedges and place onto a baking tray. Season with salt, pepper and paprika, then bake for 25 minutes.

c) Boil the kettle and place the trimmed green beans in a bowl. Pour boiling water over the green beans with a pinch of salt and allow to blanch for 1-2 minutes (do not cook fully in order to retain nutrient value).

d) Place the chicken breast on a griddle or large non-stick frying pan on a medium heat and cook until brown on one side, then flip the chicken over and flavour each breast with spices of choice

e) Once chicken is thoroughly cooked place on a board to rest and cool.

f) Drain the green beans from the salted water.

g) Once all **Ingredients** have cooled make up the the meal boxes. Add 2 handfuls of spinach, scoop of wedges, green beans and a chicken breast to each box.

h) Store in an airtight container in the fridge, then microwave for 3-4 minutes or until piping hot.

13. Asian Peanut Butter Sesame Chicken

Ingredients

For the chicken:

- 5 Tablespoon Peanut Butter
- 50ml orange juice
- 3 Tablespoon Sugar-Free Syrup (Maple Flavour)
- 3 Tablespoon soy sauce
- 1 thumb ginger (grated)
- 3 chicken breasts
- For the salad:

- 2 cucumbers (spiralised or thinly sliced)
- 2 carrots (spiralised or thinly sliced)

Salad dressing:

- 2 Tablespoon Sugar-Free Syrup (Maple Flavour) or Maple Syrup
- 4 Tablespoon soy sauce
- 2 Tablespoon sesame oil

Serve with:

- 30g (dry weight) brown/basmati rice per meal

Directions

a) Preheat the oven to 200°C or 180°C for fan-assisted.

b) Whisk peanut butter, 100ml hot water and orange juice together until smooth then add the syrup, soy sauce and ginger. Set aside.

c) Season and sear the chicken breasts by frying on a high heat using a non-stick pan for 3 minutes on each side, then transfer to a casserole dish and thoroughly coat the chicken with the peanut butter sauce.

d) Bake for 20 minutes.

e) Whilst waiting, make the salad dressing by whisking the syrup, soy, sesame oil and seeds together, then combine with the spiralised cucumber and carrots.

f) Once the chicken is cooked, place into meal prep boxes and serve with the salad and brown rice. Three days lunch prep sorted.

14. Barbecue Chicken and Rice

Ingredients

- 1 Tablespoon Coconut Oil
- 450g cooked white rice
- 600g chicken breast
- 6 handfuls spinach
- 75g sweetcorn
- 3 Tablespoon barbecue sauce
- 1 teaspoon sweet paprika
- 9 cherry tomatoes

Directions

a) Cut each raw chicken breast in half horizontally.

b) Rub the barbecue sauce, paprika, salt and pepper all over the chicken.

c) Add the coconut oil to a hot frying pan or griddle and place the chicken in the pan over a medium heat for around 4 minutes on each side. Turn over and once thoroughly cooked, place on a plate to cool.

d) Add 2 handfuls of the spinach into the base of your plastic Tupperware tubs.

e) Cook rice according to **Directions** on pack and allow to cool. Fill your tubs on one side.

f) Spoon the sweetcorn on top of the rice and add sliced tomatoes.

g) Finish the prep by adding the cold chicken and place in the fridge.

15. Low-Cal Lime and Chilli Turkey Burgers

Ingredients

- 1 teaspoon coconut oil
- 50 g rolled oats
- 40 g turkey mince (2-7% fat mince)
- 1/2 teaspoon sea salt and black pepper
- 1/2 red chilli
- 1 teaspoon garlic paste
- 1/2 small red onion
- 1/2 lime (juice and zest)

Directions

a) First, preheat oven to 180°C. Add the rolled oats to a food processor and process until finely blended.

b) Add the onion, chilli, garlic, and lime juice and zest and process until coarsely chopped. Next, add the burger mince, salt and pepper and pulse to combine.

c) Make 5 burger patties with your hands and place onto a lined baking tray.

d) Bake for 15-20 minutes.

e) Serve with vegetables of choice.

16. Malaysian Chicken Satay

Makes: 4 meals

Ingredients

- 2 Tablespoon sesame, peanut, or olive oil
- 2 stalks lemongrass
- 1 white onion
- 2 cloves garlic
- 1 thumb ginger
- 2 red chillies
- 1 teaspoon turmeric
- 1 teaspoon cumin seeds
- 8 Tablespoon Powdered Peanut Butter or 4-6 Tablespoon regular Peanut Butter
- 3 chicken breasts (diced)
- 300g wholegrain rice (cooked)
- 1 red onion (chopped)
- 1 cucumber (chopped)

Directions

a) First, place the sesame oil, lemongrass, onion, garlic, ginger, chillies, turmeric and cumin into a blender. Process until you get a smooth paste.

b) Next, in a separate bowl, mix 8 Tablespoon Powdered Peanut Butter with 8 Tablespoon water until it looks like peanut butter. Add a little more powder or water to get your desired consistency.

c) Combine half of the spice paste with the peanut butter to make a peanut sauce, and pour the remaining spice paste over your diced chicken. Thread the chicken onto 6 small skewers (soak your skewers in water for at least an hour so that the wood doesn't burn). Allow the chicken to marinate for a couple of hours if you have time.

d) Fry the chicken skewers on a medium to high heat for 8-10 minutes or until completely cooked through. Once cooked, remove from the pan and set aside.

e) Add the peanut sauce to the same pan and bring to the boil, stirring occasionally until piping hot. Remove from the heat.

f) Prepare three Tupperware boxes with cooked rice, chopped cucumber and chopped red onion. Add two chicken skewers to each box. Divide the peanut sauce into three smaller Tupperware boxes or pour the sauce straight over the chicken.

g) Refrigerate for up to 3 days. Microwave on full power for 3 minutes or until piping hot. And there you go – 3 days' worth of meals to liven up your office lunches!

17. Chicken Tikka Masala

Serves 4

Ingredients

- 1 Tablespoon 100% Coconut Oil
- 500g chicken breast (diced)
- 1 white onion (finely chopped)
- 4 garlic cloves (grated or crushed)
- 1 Tablespoon ginger (grated)
- 2 Tablespoon tomato puree
- 1 teaspoon turmeric
- 1 teaspoon garam masala
- $\frac{1}{2}$ teaspoon chilli powder
- 1 tin chopped tomatoes (blended)
- 1 mug of boiling chicken stock
- 3 large Tablespoon full-fat Greek yoghurt

Serve with:

- 50g basmati rice per serving (dry weight)
- 2 flatbreads (cut into strips)
- 20g chopped cashews

Directions

a) First, heat the coconut oil in a pan over a medium heat and add the chicken breast and onion. Season with salt and pepper, then fry until chicken is no longer pink on the outside.

b) Reduce your heat and add the garlic, ginger, tomato paste, turmeric, garam masala, and chilli powder, along with a splash of water and stir well for 1-2 minutes to allow the fragrances from the spices to release.

c) Then, add the blended tomatoes and chicken stock, bring your pan to simmer and leave to simmer for 10 minutes, stirring occasionally.

d) Once your sauce has reduced by roughly half, take off the heat and stir through the Greek yoghurt. If you want it super-creamy, feel free to add more Greek yoghurt or vice versa.

e) Serve with basmati rice, flatbread strips, and chopped cashews.

18. One-Pot Coconut Chicken and Rice Meal Prep

Ingredients

For the chicken:

- 5-6 skinless chicken thighs
- 2 Tablespoon yoghurt
- 1 teaspoon ginger
- 1 teaspoon turmeric
- $\frac{1}{2}$ teaspoon chilli powder
- $\frac{1}{4}$ teaspoon salt

For the pot:

- 1 Tablespoon coconut oil
- 1 onion (thinly sliced)
- 2-3 garlic cloves (grated)
- 1 teaspoon ginger (grated)
- $\frac{1}{2}$ teaspoon chilli powder
- 250g basmati rice (soaked and drained)
- 1 can light coconut milk
- $\frac{1}{2}$ large mug of boiled water

To serve:

- Chopped cashews
- Coriander

Directions

a) Add the chicken thighs, yoghurt, ginger, turmeric, chilli powder, and salt to a bowl and mix well until the chicken is completely coated. Set aside and leave to marinade at least 15 minutes, preferably overnight.

b) Heat coconut oil in a large deep pan or casserole dish on a medium heat and add the chicken thighs.

c) Cook for 5 minutes before flipping and cooking for a further 5-10 minutes until chicken is cooked through. Remove from the pan and set aside.

d) Add the onion to the pan with a small splash of water and fry for 5 minutes. Then add the garlic, ginger, chilli powder, and another splash of water. Stir constantly until the onion is coated in spices and leave to fry for 2 minutes.

e) Stir the basmati rice into the onion and spices, then add the coconut milk and 1/2 a mug of boiled water. Give it all a good stir, bring to a simmer, and then place the chicken thighs back into the pan on top of the rice.

f) Cover with a lid and leave to cook for 15-20 minutes, until rice is cooked.

g) Garnish with chopped cashews and coriander before serving.

19. BBQ Pulled Chicken Mac N Cheese

Serves 4

Ingredients

For the BBQ pulled chicken:

- 4 Tablespoon Sugar-Free Sauce (BBQ)
- 1 teaspoon paprika
- 1 teaspoon garlic granules
- Salt
- Pepper
- 300g chicken breast

For the mac n cheese:

- 3 Tablespoon butter
- 3 Tablespoon plain flour
- 1 garlic clove (crushed)
- 1 Tablespoon paprika
- 1-pint semi-skimmed milk
- 150g low-fat cheddar (grated)
- 250g macaroni pasta
- Chilli flakes to season

Directions

a) Preheat the oven to 180°C/350°F and boil a large saucepan of water.

b) Then, mix together the BBQ Sugar-Free Sauce, paprika, garlic granules, salt, and pepper in a small bowl.

c) Slice deep cuts sideways into each chicken breast and transfer them to a baking tray lined with foil. Then pour the BBQ sauce mixture onto the chicken breasts.

d) Rub the sauce into the chicken breast so that they are completely covered, then seal the chicken breasts in the foil and bake for 25 minutes.

e) Once baked, remove the chicken from the foil – set the BBQ juices aside — and then shred the chicken using two forks.

f) Add the BBQ juices and shredded chicken to a pan fry over medium heat for 3-4 minutes, then set aside. Feel free to add some more BBQ Sugar-Free Sauce if you wish.

g) Put your macaroni pasta on to cook.

h) Meanwhile, melt the butter in a deep pan. Add the garlic and paprika and sauté for 2 minutes.

i) Add the flour, whisking well, and then gradually add the milk.

j) Then, add the low-fat cheddar, stirring until it melts into the white sauce, and then finally add your shredded BBQ chicken and cooked macaroni pasta. Stir well to make sure everything is combined.

k) Serve with a sprinkle of chilli flakes or black pepper for a little kick, and enjoy!

20. Peanut Butter Chicken Curry

Serves 4

Ingredients

- 1 Tablespoon 100% Coconut Oil
- 400g chicken breast (cubed)
- 1 onion (sliced)
- 2 garlic cloves (finely chopped)
- 1 thumb-sized piece ginger (finely chopped)
- 1 red chilli (deseeded and finely chopped)
- 5 Tablespoon curry powder
- 1 tin chopped tomatoes
- 1 handful fresh coriander (chopped)
- 400ml light coconut milk
- 100g All-Natural Peanut Butter (Crunchy)

To serve:

- Basmati rice (around 75g per person)
- Chopped peanuts
- Coriander

Directions

a) First, heat the coconut oil in a large pan and add the chicken. Season lightly and fry until cooked through and golden brown on the outside, then set aside.

b) Now, add the onion and fry until soft. Add the chopped garlic, ginger, and chilli and fry for another 1-2 minutes before adding the curry powder and a large splash of water. Bring to a simmer, stir well and cook for 5 minutes.

c) Now, add the chopped tomatoes and coriander, give it a good stir and leave to simmer for another 10 minutes, stirring occasionally.

d) Gradually stir in the light coconut milk to the sauce and then add your crunchy peanut butter. Give it all really good stir, and leave to simmer on a low heat until your curry has reached your desired consistency.

e) Serve with basmati rice and a sprinkling of chopped coriander and peanuts, then enjoy!

21. Fajita Pasta Bake

Serves 5

Ingredients

- 1 Tablespoon coconut oil
- 350g chicken thigh (cubed)
- 1 onion (finely sliced)
- 2 bell peppers (finely sliced)
- ½ pack fajita seasoning
- 350g rigatoni
- 100g salsa dip
- 100g light cream cheese
- A small bunch of coriander (stems removed, finely chopped)
- 50g light cheddar
- 30g light mozzarella

Directions

a) First, preheat the oven to 180°C/ 360°C.

b) Heat the coconut oil in a large pan and add your chicken thighs. Season well with salt and pepper and fry for 6-7 minutes, flipping once or twice, until they start to brown on the outside. Remove from pan and set aside.

c) Get your pasta on so it's ready to add to the pan in ten minutes.

d) Now, add the onion and peppers to the pan and fry until soft, stirring regularly. Add the fajita seasoning and the cooked chicken back in, stir well and fry for 5 minutes.

e) Then, add your cooked pasta (make sure to drain it before), the salsa, and the cream cheese and mix thoroughly so everything is evenly combined.

f) Finally, add your chopped coriander and stir well before transferring to a large baking dish.

g) Top with your cheese and bake for 10-15 minutes until it starts to turn crispy.

h) Garnish with chopped spring onions and coriander, then dig in!

22. Creamy Lemon and Thyme Chicken

Serves 6

Ingredients

- 2 teaspoon fresh thyme
- 2 teaspoon mixed herbs
- Salt and pepper to taste
- 6 boneless, skinless chicken thighs
- 1 Tablespoon oil
- 1 onion (chopped)
- 2 garlic cloves (chopped)
- Juice of 1 lemon
- 100ml chicken stock
- 200ml crème fraiche
- Lemon slices
- Fresh thyme

Serving suggestions:

- Quinoa (around 50g per serving)
- Tender stem broccoli

Directions

a) First, prepare the seasoning by mixing the fresh thyme, mixed herbs, salt, and pepper in a little bowl. Sprinkle generously over your chicken thighs, making sure to coat evenly, and keep any remaining seasoning to the side to use later.

b) Next, add the oil to a large pan over a medium heat. Once hot, add your chicken thighs and cook for several minutes on each side. They should be crispy and browned on the outside, and completely cooked through on the inside (with no pink bits). Remove the chicken from the pan and set aside.

c) In the same pan as you cooked the chicken, add the onion and garlic and cook for a few minutes until softened. Then add the lemon juice, chicken stock, and any of the remaining seasoning mix, stir well to combine, and allow to bubble for a few minutes.

d) Add the crème fraiche, stir through, and cook for another 2-3 minutes to thicken. Then add the chicken thighs back into the pan and allow to heat up for a few minutes.

e) Remove from the heat and garnish with fresh lemon slices and a sprinkle of thyme. Serve up with quinoa and enjoy immediately or portion up for your meal prep for the week. Delicious.

23. Chicken and Chorizo Paella

Serves 5

Ingredients

- 100g chorizo
- 500g skinless chicken thighs
- Salt and pepper to taste
- 1 onion (chopped)
- 1 teaspoon turmeric
- 1 teaspoon paprika
- 2 garlic cloves (minced)
- 1 red pepper (sliced)
- 225g paella rice
- 400ml chicken stock
- 4 tomatoes (chopped)
- 100g peas

To garnish:

- Lemon and lime wedges
- Fresh parsley

Directions

a) First add the chorizo pieces to a large non-stick pan and cook for a few minutes until the sides begin to brown and oils are released. Then remove and set aside for later.

b) Add the chicken thighs to the pan and cook in the natural oils from the chorizo. Season with salt and pepper and cook through until browned on each side and no pink remains. Remove from the pan and set aside too.

c) Next, add the chopped onion and fry for a few minutes until softened. Then add the turmeric, paprika, garlic, and red pepper, stirring well to coat everything in the spices.

d) After a couple of minutes, add the paella rice and stir through. Then pour in the chicken stock and chopped tomatoes and mix everything until evenly combined.

e) Add the chorizo pieces back into the pan and stir through, then add the chicken thighs. Cover the pan with a lid and simmer for 15 minutes to allow the rice to cook and soak up the liquid.

f) Finally add the peas, stir through, and allow to warm for a few final minutes before taking off the heat. Serve up with plenty of lime and lemon wedges and a garnish of fresh parsley.

24. Easy Protein Bowl Meal Prep

Serves 1

Ingredients

- 2 Tablespoon soy sauce
- 1 Tablespoon honey
- 1 teaspoon black pepper
- 1 Tablespoon garlic (minced)
- 1 chicken breast
- 75g quinoa
- 200ml water
- 1 egg
- 50g broccoli
- 50g mangetout
- ½ red pepper (sliced)
- 4 cherry tomatoes (halved)
- Spring onions (chopped)

Directions

a) First, mix together the soy sauce, honey, black pepper, and garlic to make a marinade. Pour 3/4s of the marinade over the chicken breast, cover, and leave to marinate in the fridge for 30 minutes (or you could do this the night before). Keep the remaining marinade aside for serving with later.

b) Next, add the quinoa and 200ml water to a pan, cover with the lid, and bring to the boil. Once boiling, add a sieve over the pan and place your egg in the centre above the quinoa. Cover again and let steam for 10 minutes.

c) Meanwhile in a separate frying pan, heat a little oil or low-calorie cooking spray and then add your marinated chicken breast. Cook for around 5-7 minutes on each side until browned and completely cooked through with no pink bits inside.

d) Add the broccoli and mangetout to the sieve above the quinoa, then cover and steam for a further 5 minutes. Then carefully remove the sieve and stir the quinoa with a fork to fluff up.

e) Build your protein bowl. Make a quinoa base, then add the cooked broccoli and mangetout, along with slices of red pepper and cherry tomatoes. Add the sliced chicken breast and boiled egg (remove the shell first!) then add the remaining marinade that you kept aside and garnish with chopped spring onion.

25. Seared Tuna Steak and Sweet Potato Wedges

Makes 4

Ingredients

For the tuna steaks:

- 4 x 150g tuna steaks
- 1 teaspoon coarse sea salt
- 1 Tablespoon 100% Coconut Oil (melted)
- 2 Tablespoon pink peppercorns
- For the sweet potatoes:
- 4 large sweet potatoes
- 1 Tablespoon plain flour
- 1/2 teaspoon salt
- 1/2 teaspoon pepper
- 1/2 Tablespoon 100% Coconut Oil (melted)

Directions

a) First, preheat your oven to 200°C.

b) Then, prepare the sweet potatoes. Scrub clean each potato and prick all over with a fork. Place onto a microwavable plate and microwave on high for 4-5 minutes, then remove from the microwave and allow to cool for a minute or two.

c) Once cool enough to touch, cut the sweet potatoes into wedges. Sprinkle the flour, salt, pepper and melted coconut oil over the wedges and shake them about a little to coat them (this will make them super-crispy). Pop them onto a baking tray and bake at 200°C for 15-20 minutes.

d) When the sweet potato fries are nearly ready, it's time to cook your tuna steaks. Coat each steak with melted coconut oil on both sides, then sprinkle with salt, and place in a large frying or griddle pan that's already been over the heat for a minute or so.

e) Fry the tuna steaks on each side for a 1-2 minutes if you prefer seared tuna, or 3-4 minutes on each side if you prefer it cooked through.

f) Prepare your meal prep boxes with a bed of salad or spinach leaves, then divide up the sweet potato wedges and finally add a tuna steak. Sprinkle the steak with crushed pink peppercorns and serve with a lemon wedge.

g) Store in airtight containers in the refrigerator for up to 3 days. When ready to eat, remove the lid and place it loosely back on top, leaving a little gap. Microwave on high for $3\frac{1}{2}$ minutes or until piping hot. Allow to stand for 1 minute before eating.

26. Quick Spicy Cajun Salmon and Garlicky Veg

Ingredients

- 3 cloves garlic (roughly chopped)
- 1 lemon (sliced into very thin rings)
- 3 wild salmon fillets
- 1.5 Tablespoon cajun seasoning
- 1 Tablespoon olive oil
- 1 teaspoon coarse sea salt and black pepper
- 180g (dry weight) couscous
- 10-12 stems tender stem broccoli
- 2 courgettes

Directions

a) Preheat oven to 160°C. Chop the dry ends of the tender stem broccoli off (about 1cm) and spiralise the courgette.

b) Lay the broccoli out into a deep baking tray, then layer with the courgette, garlic, and lemon and season with sea salt and black pepper. Drizzle with a little olive oil.

c) Rub the salmon fillets on all sides with the remaining olive oil and the cajun seasoning, then place them on top on the vegetables, skin-side up. Bake for 25 minutes, then increase the temperature to 180°C and bake for a further 5 minutes, until the skin begins to crisp up.

d) Cook couscous according to **Directions** on the pack, then divide amongst 3 Tupperware containers. Divide the salmon, vegetables and some lemon slices amongst the containers and allow to cool. Cover and refrigerate for up to 3 days.

e) When ready to eat, microwave on full power for 3 minutes or until piping hot.

27. Tuna Pasta Salad

Serves 3

Ingredients

- 200g cooked pasta
- 2 cans tuna
- 1 tin sweetcorn (100g)
- 2 carrots (shredded)
- 1 yellow pepper (diced)

For the dressing:

- 4 Tablespoon olive oil
- 1 lemon (juice and zest)
- ½ teaspoon garlic powder
- Salt and pepper to taste

Directions

a) First, make the dressing by adding the oil, lemon juice and zest, garlic powder, and salt and pepper to a small bowl and mixing well.

b) Next, add your cooked pasta to a large bowl and then add the shredded carrot, sweetcorn, diced pepper, and drained tuna. Pour the dressing over the top and then use a large spoon to carefully mix everything together so it's all evenly distributed.

c) Portion up into 3 meal prep containers and store in the fridge for the next few days. Lunch sorted.

28. Salmon Poke Bowl

Serves 4

Ingredients

- 3 Tablespoon light mayonnaise
- 1 Tablespoon sriracha
- 2 Tablespoon soy sauce
- 2 Tablespoon mirin (or any other rice wine vinegar)
- 1 Tablespoon toasted sesame oil
- 1 Tablespoon honey
- 300 g sashimi grade salmon
- 1 carrot
- 1 cucumber
- 2-3 spring onions
- 1 avocado (sliced)
- 1 cup ready-to-eat edamame beans
- 250 g sticky white sushi rice
- 1-2 shallots (finely sliced)
- 1 Tablespoon coconut oil
- To garnish: sesame seeds

Directions

a) First, mix together the light mayonnaise, sriracha, soy sauce, mirin, sesame oil, and honey to make a smooth marinade.

b) Reserve $\frac{1}{2}$ the marinade to use as a dressing later, then add sashimi salmon to remaining marinade. Mix salmon together with marinade, being careful not to damage it, then leave to marinate for at least one hour.

c) Rinse sushi rice thoroughly until the water runs clear. Then, cook sushi rice according to packet **Directions** (usually cook for around 10 minutes and then steam for 10 minutes) and leave to cool before serving.

d) Chop your cucumber into quarters, thinly slice the spring onions lengthways, and julienne carrots using a peeler.

e) Now heat the coconut oil in a non-stick pan and add sliced shallots. Gently sauté the shallots on low heat for approximately 7 minutes, until they turn brown and crispy. Then remove from pan and transfer to a piece of paper kitchen towel.

f) Once, everything is ready, build your poke bowl, by layering rice first then all your toppings. Garnish with sesame seeds and enjoy immediately, or keep in airtight containers in the fridge for up to 3 days as meal prep.

29. High-Protein Kedgeree

Makes: 3 meals

Ingredients

- 3 fillets smoked haddock
- 1 teaspoon Coconut Oil
- 1 white onion (finely chopped)
- 1 teaspoon turmeric
- 1 teaspoon ground coriander
- 1 teaspoon medium curry powder
- 3 hard-boiled eggs (peeled and quartered)
- 500g cooked wholegrain rice or Zero Rice (160g dry weight)
- Handful fresh coriander

Directions

a) Place the smoked haddock into a large frying pan over a medium heat. Cover with an inch of water. Bring to the boil then turn the heat down and simmer for 5 minutes. Once cooked, remove from the heat and break apart into chunks. Set aside.

b) Pour the water out of the pan and add the coconut oil. Add the chopped onion and simmer over a medium to low heat for 5 minutes until golden.

c) Add the turmeric, ground coriander and curry powder and cook for a further 30 seconds, stirring occasionally.

d) Add the cooked rice and haddock and stir. Heat through, then add the boiled eggs and stir again. Transfer to meal-prep containers and serve with your choice of vegetables.

30. Spiced Lamb With Feta Bulgur

Serves 2

Ingredients

- 1 Tablespoon oil
- 1 red onion (sliced)
- 1 Tablespoon ras el hanout
- 3 Tablespoon tomato puree
- 250g lamb mince
- Salt and pepper to taste
- 125ml boiling water
- 130g bulgur wheat
- 100g feta (cubed)
- ½ cucumber (sliced into chunks)
- Fresh mint leaves to garnish

Directions

a) First, heat the oil in a large frying pan and cook the onion for a few minutes until softened. Add the ras el hanout and tomato puree and stir until everything is evenly coated.

b) Now add the lamb mince and break up into pieces, stirring to combine with everything else. Season with salt and pepper to taste and let cook for 5-10 minutes or until no longer pink.

c) Add the boiling water and leave to simmer for a further 10 minutes so that the liquid reduces and the sauce thickens.

d) Meanwhile, add the bulgur wheat to a pan of boiling water and cook as per the package directions.

e) Once cooked, fluff up with a fork and add the cubes of feta and cucumber, mixing through the bulgur.

f) Build a bed of feta bulgur on a plate and add a few spoonfuls of the lamb mixture on top.

g) Garnish with a few fresh mint leaves and then serve up!

31. Lean, Creamy Sausage Pasta

Servings 4 portions

Ingredients

- 1 teaspoon 100% Coconut Oil
- 1 leek (finely sliced)
- 2 clove garlic cloves(chopped)
- 8 reduced-fat sausages (sliced)
- 200 g quark
- 1 tin chopped tomatoes
- 240 g wholemeal penne pasta
- 1 teaspoon dried chilli flakes
- 1 pinch of salt and pepper to taste
- 1 handful fresh basil leaves

Directions

a) Add the coconut oil to a large, non-stick pan on a medium to high heat. Add the sliced leek into the pan and fry for 3-4 minutes, stirring occasionally.

b) Add the garlic and pan fry for a further 2 minutes, then add the sliced sausages and fry for 6-10 minutes, stirring occasionally, until they are brown on all sides. Add the chilli flakes and season with salt and pepper to taste.

c) Next, the tin of tomatoes and stir to combine. Let bubble for a few minutes and then add the quark, mixing through thoroughly to get a rich, creamy sauce.

d) Add the cooked pasta to the pan and mix in with the sauce so that it's all combined.

e) After a few minutes, take the pasta off the heat and portion up into containers, garnishing with fresh basil leaves.

32. Sweet Potato and Chorizo Hash

Servings: 4

Ingredients

- 500g sweet potatoes
- 1 Tablespoon Coconut Oil
- ½ red onion (finely chopped)
- 200g tinned chickpeas (drained)
- 150g chorizo or pancetta (chopped into 1cm cubes)
- ½ teaspoon sea salt
- ½ teaspoon black pepper
- 4 medium free-range eggs
- Handful pickled and sliced jalapeños

Directions

a) Peel the sweet potatoes and chop into 2cm cubes. Put the cubes into a pan and cover with water, then bring to the boil. Once boiling, drain and allow the steam to run off for 2-3 minutes.

b) While waiting, add the coconut oil to a pan on a medium to high heat. Once melted, add the chopped onions and chorizo/pancetta, and fry for 3-4 minutes, stirring occasionally.

c) Next, turn the heat down to medium and add the sweet potatoes, chickpeas, jalapenos, sea salt and black pepper. Squash them down a little and fry for 8-10 minutes without moving them, until the bottom becomes crispy.

d) Once crispy, make 4 small wells in the hash and break in the eggs. Cover the pan with a lid and cook for 2-3 minutes until the eggs are cooked but the yolk is still runny (you can cook for longer if you like your yolks well-done).

e) Top with a few extra jalapeños and serve.

33. Teriyaki Beef Zoodles

Makes: 4 meals

Ingredients

For the sauce:

- 75ml soy sauce
- 120ml water
- 1.5 Tablespoon cornstarch
- 4-5 Tablespoon Organic Maple Syrup
- Optional: 1 clove garlic (chopped)
- ½ thumb ginger (grated)

For the rest:

- 1 teaspoon Coconut Oil
- 3 rump steaks (cut into slices)
- 4 courgettes (spiralised)
- 2 yellow peppers (chopped)
- 75g edamame beans
- Sprinkle sesame seeds

Directions

a) Whisk soy, water and cornstarch/guar gum in a saucepan and heat gently for 5-6 minutes until the sauce has thickened. Add the garlic and ginger at this point if you're using it. Once thickened, whisk in the maple syrup and remove from the heat. Set aside.

b) Heat a large wok (or pan) on high for 1-2 minutes. When it's really hot, add the coconut oil and steak slices and sauté for 1-2 minutes, flipping occasionally.

c) Add the spiralised courgette and chopped pepper and stir-fry for a further 2-3 minutes.

d) Finally, stir through the teriyaki sauce and edamame beans then transfer to Tupperware boxes and allow to cool.

e) Sprinkle a few sesame seeds over each and refrigerate. Easy!

34. Baked Feta Couscous

Serves 4

Ingredients

- 200g feta
- 400g cherry tomatoes
- 1 teaspoon mixed herbs
- 1 Tablespoon olive oil
- 200g couscous
- 500ml vegetable stock
- Fresh chillies to garnish
- Parsley to garnish

Directions

a) Preheat the oven to 200°C.

b) Add the feta and cherry tomatoes to an ovenproof baking dish. Sprinkle with mixed herbs and drizzle with olive oil, then bake in the oven for 25-30 minutes.

c) Meanwhile, add the couscous to a large bowl and cover with boiling vegetable stock. Mix well, cover with a lid or plate, then leave to cook for around 10 minutes or until the liquid has been soaked up and the couscous is light and fluffy.

d) Now, with a fork or masher, lightly mash the baked feta and cherry tomatoes until all combined in a kind of thick sauce. Add the couscous and stir to combine.

e) Garnish with chopped fresh chillies, a crack of black pepper, and parsley leaves. Enjoy immediately or keep for up to 3 days.

35. One-Pot Lentil Dahl

Makes 4

Ingredients

- 2 Tablespoon 100% Coconut Oil
- 1 Onion (chopped)
- 1 inch Ginger
- 3 garlic cloves (crushed)
- 1.5 Tablespoon turmeric
- 1.5 Tablespoon cumin
- 1.5 Tablespoon medium curry powder
- 300 g red lentils (washed)
- 1 Tin chopped tomatoes
- 1.2 litre vegetable stock
- 1 Coriander
- 200 g plain flour
- 1/4 Tablespoon salt
- 2 teaspoon baking powder
- 250 g plain dairy-free yoghurt

Directions

a) First, add the coconut oil to a large sauce pan on a medium heat. Once melted, add the onion, ginger and garlic, and fry for 3-4 minutes, stirring occasionally.

b) While waiting, prepare the stock in a separate bowl or jug — dissolving a stock cube in 1200ml boiling water. Set aside.

c) Then add the turmeric, cumin and curry powder to the frying pan and fry for a further minute while stirring.

d) Add the lentils and stir to make sure that they're fully combined with the **Ingredients** already in the pan. Then add the tomatoes and mix through.

e) Now carefully pour in the stock, stirring slowly to make sure everything is fully combined. Lower the heat, place the lid on the pan and then leave to simmer for 30 minutes.

f) While waiting, start to prepare your naans. Add the flour, salt, baking powder and yoghurt to a bowl and mix well until you have a thick dough.

g) Sprinkle a little flour over your work surface and then use your hands to fully knead and combine the dough into a ball. Use a sharp knife to cut the ball into equal sections — we went for 8 sections for mini naans, but quarters would make 4 big ones.

h) Shape each section of dough into a flat disc shape with your hands, and then place them into a frying pan over medium heat, one at a time. Fry for a few minutes on each so, until it begins to rise up and brown.

i) Once your one-pot lentil dahl has cooked, stir well and then portion up with rice into meal prep containers. Add a mini naan to each one and garnish with coriander.

36. Sweet Paprika Vegan Bowl and Chocolate Protein Balls

Ingredients

Ingredients

- 2 400g firm tofu
- 400 g chickpeas
- 1 Tablespoon Coconut Oil
- 1 Tablespoon paprika
- 200 g asparagus
- 1 pinch sea salt and pepper
- 1 large sweet potato
- 1 Tablespoon flour
- 1 Tablespoon Organic Maca Powder

For the avocado cream:

- 2 small ripe avocados
- 2 Tablespoon apple cider vinegar
- 2 Tablespoon extra-virgin olive oil
- 1-2 Tablespoon cold water
- Pinch sea salt and pepper

For the protein balls:

- 2 scoops Vegan Blend (Chocolate Smooth Flavour)
- 2 scoops Instant Oats
- 75g Cashew Butter
- 2 Tablespoon Sugar-Free Syrup/honey/agave
- 1-2 Tablespoon almond/coconut/soy milk
- 1 Tablespoon chia seeds for rolling

Directions

a) Preheat oven to 200°C or 180°C for fan-assisted.

b) Peel sweet potatoes and cut into skinny fries, then parboil for 10 minutes. Drain well and leave for a few minutes to release moisture, then sprinkle over a little flour and 1 Tablespoon maca powder. Bake for 20-25 minutes on the top shelf of the oven.

c) Whilst waiting, heat a large pan on a medium to high heat and add coconut oil, chickpeas and asparagus. Fry for 7-8 minutes and then add the tofu. Fry for a further 3 minutes, tossing occasionally and add paprika, salt and pepper and fry for 2 more minutes.

For the avocado cream:

d) Add all **Ingredients** to a blender and process until smooth and creamy. Place into a small Tupperware box to add to your meal prep once you've warmed it up again.

For the protein balls:

e) Combine the Vegan Blend and Instant Oats in a mixing bowl. Add the nut butter and syrup, mix, and gradually add the milk until you can roll the mixture into balls. Roll the balls in chia seeds and pop into plastic tubs to bring with you for a healthy snack!

37. Ultimate 15-Minute Vegan Fajitas

Serves: 2

Ingredients

- 1 Tablespoon Coconut Oil
- 2 bell peppers (sliced)
- 1 white onion (sliced)
- 4 Portobello mushrooms (sliced)
- Fajita seasoning spices: $\frac{1}{2}$ teaspoon paprika, 1 teaspoon chilli powder, $\frac{1}{2}$ teaspoon garlic powder, $\frac{1}{2}$ teaspoon cumin
- 1 Tablespoon soy sauce
- Good handful pickled and sliced jalapeño peppers
- 6 small whole wheat tortillas

Optional toppings:

- Guacamole
- Tomato salsa

Directions

a) Heat a large pan on a medium to high heat. Drop in the coconut oil, then once it has melted, add the sliced onions and bell peppers. Fry for 8-10 minutes until the vegetables begin to soften, then stir through the spices and fry for a further 2 minutes, stirring occasionally.

b) Add the Portobello mushrooms and soy sauce to the mixture and fry until browned – this should take around 4-6 minutes.

c) Once browned, warm the tortillas in the oven for 5-10 minutes or in the microwave on full power for 30 seconds. Fill the tortillas with your Portobello fajita mix, and top with jalapeño peppers, guacamole and salsa. Perfection.

38. Crispy Tofu and Teriyaki Noodles

Serves 4

Ingredients

For the teriyaki sauce:

- 70ml soy sauce
- 2 Tablespoon brown sugar
- 1 teaspoon ginger (finely chopped)
- 1 teaspoon garlic (finely chopped)
- 1 teaspoon sesame seed oil
- 1 Tablespoon honey
- 3 Tablespoon mirin
- 2 teaspoon cornflour (mixed with a splash of cold water)

For the crispy tofu:

- 1 block tofu
- 3 Tablespoon soy sauce
- 50g cornflour
- 1 Tablespoon coconut oil

For the stir fry:

- 1 Tablespoon coconut oil
- 1 carrot (cut into matchsticks)
- 1 broccoli (florets cut from stem)
- 4 nests of egg noodles
- To garnish: spring onions (chopped)

Directions

a) First, make the teriyaki sauce by mixing the soy sauce, brown sugar, garlic, ginger, sesame seed oil, honey, mirin (or rice wine vinegar), and cornflour mixture together in a small bowl. Stir well so that all the **Ingredients** combine evenly.

b) Next, add 3 tablespoons of soy sauce and 50g of cornflour to two separate bowls. Dice your tofu, then dip each piece in soy sauce, then cornflour, making sure each bit is coated before setting aside.

c) Heat the coconut oil in a non-stick pan or wok, then add coated tofu to pan to cook, stirring and flipping every 1-2 minutes, until crispy and golden brown. Remove and set aside.

d) Boil a large saucepan of water and cook your egg noodles according to package directions.

e) Then, heat remaining coconut oil in pan and add the carrot and broccoli. Stir fry for 5 minutes, until slightly soft, then remove from pan.

f) Add teriyaki sauce to pan, cook on a low heat until sauce starts to bubble and thicken. Once you're happy with the consistency of the sauce, add the drained egg noodles to pan. Toss noodles to coat in teriyaki sauce, then add in carrot and broccoli, and toss to combine.

g) Divide teriyaki noodles between 4 meal prep boxes, serve crispy tofu on top, and garnish with spring onions. Sorted.

39. Vegan Lentil Bolognese

Serves 4

Ingredients

- 1 Tablespoon olive oil
- 1 onion (diced)
- 2 carrots (diced)
- 2 celery stalks (diced)
- 3 garlic cloves (minced)
- Seasoning: salt and pepper
- 2 Tablespoon tomato puree
- 120 g red lentils (dry weight)
- 1 tin chopped tomatoes
- 300 ml water
- 1 vegetable stock cube
- Serve with: penne pasta and fresh basil

Directions

a) Heat the olive oil in a large pan and add the onion. Fry for a few minutes to soften, then add the carrot and stir through.

b) Add the diced celery and cook everything for 5 minutes before adding the minced garlic and diced mushrooms. Stir to combine all **Ingredients** in the pan, season generously, and cook for another 2-3 minutes until the mushrooms are browned.

c) Next stir in the tomato puree, then the red lentils and chopped tomatoes.

d) Carefully add the water to the pan, making sure to cover everything, and then stir in the vegetable stock cube. Leave to simmer over a low heat for 20 minutes until the lentils have absorbed most of the water and doubled in size.

e) Serve immediately on a bed of freshly cooked pasta or spaghetti and garnish with fresh basil.

f) Portion up any remaining servings into meal prep containers to enjoy later in the week.

40. Breakfast Burritos For All Week Long

Makes: 5

Ingredients

- 150g long grain or brown rice (dry weight)
- 100g tinned chopped tomatoes
- 1 large white onion (finely chopped)
- 10 medium eggs or 250ml liquid egg whites
- 10 reduced-fat pork sausages (chopped into 1cm cubes)
- 125g reduced-fat cheddar or Mexican-style cheese (grated)
- 250g tinned black beans
- 1 teaspoon sea salt, black pepper and smoked paprika
- 5 wholemeal tortillas
- 50g pickled and sliced jalapenos

Directions

a) First, boil the rice. Pour the dry rice into a large saucepan and cover with 200ml cold water and the chopped tomatoes. Bring to the boil, then turn the heat down to low, cover with a lid and simmer for 10-15 minutes until the rice has absorbed all the liquid.

b) While you're waiting for the rice to boil, cook the rest. Place a large, non-stick pan on a medium to high heat with a little coconut oil. Once the coconut oil has melted, add the chopped onion and fry for 3-4 minutes until the onions begin to brown.

c) Add the sausage cubes and black beans to the pan with the paprika, salt and pepper, and fry for a further 3-4 minutes until crispy. Once cooked, pour into a bowl and set aside, and return the pan to the heat.

d) Once the sausage mixture has cooked, fry the eggs. Crack the eggs into a bowl with a little salt and pepper, and whisk using a fork. Pour the eggs into the pan and fry for 3-4 minutes while stirring.

e) Once all the components are cooked, assemble your burritos. Lay the tortillas out flat and divide the cooked rice into the middle of each in a short, thick line, leaving space around the edges. Add the sausage, onion and black bean mixture on top, then the eggs, grated cheese, and finally the jalapenos.

f) Now fold the burritos. Fold the sides of each tortilla over the middle of the mixture, then fold the bottom edge tightly up to the middle. Roll the wrapped mixture tightly upwards towards the only open edge, and continue to roll until you have a tight burrito.

g) Time to freeze the burritos. Wrap each burrito tightly with cling film and pop them into the freezer.

h) When you're ready to eat a healthy breakfast burrito, simply unwrap the burrito and wrap it with a piece of kitchen towel, then microwave for approx. 2 minutes or until hot through. Add half an avocado once warmed if you like.

41. Burrito Jars

Ingredients

- 4 chicken breasts
- 1 teaspoon Coconut Oil
- 4 tomatoes (finely chopped)
- 1 red onion (finely chopped)
- Pinch salt and pepper
- 1 lime (juiced)
- 4 sachets (400g) Zero Rice
- 1 200g tin sweetcorn (drained)
- 2 avocados
- 2 heads little gem lettuce (chopped)
- 8 Tablespoon soured cream
- Spring onions to garnish

Directions

a) Cut chicken breasts into cubes, season, and pan fry on a medium heat with a little coconut oil until fully cooked through. Remove and allow to cool.

b) Cook the rice. Rinse under cold water, and then cook for either 1 minute in the microwave or 2-3 minutes in a pan. Set aside and allow to cool a little.

c) Assemble your mason jars. Divide and drop in the chopped tomatoes and onions, lime juice and a little salt and pepper and mix. Add 2 Tablespoon soured cream to each jar. By adding the liquid first, you won't get a soggy salad after a few days in the fridge.

d) Divide the sweetcorn amongst the jars, then add the rice, chicken, avocado, little gem lettuce leaves and lastly the cheese. Screw on the lid and enjoy 4 days' worth of healthy lunches!

42. Ultimate High-Protein Stuffed Peppers 4 Ways

Ingredients

- 2 large bell peppers, tops and seeds removed
- 50g long grain rice, cooked
- 1 chicken breast (cooked and chopped)
- 2 Tablespoon tomato salsa
- 50g black beans
- 1 sachet fajita spice (or to make your own, combine $\frac{1}{2}$ teaspoon paprika, $\frac{1}{2}$ teaspoon onion powder, $\frac{1}{2}$ teaspoon garlic powder, $\frac{1}{4}$ teaspoon salt, $\frac{1}{4}$ teaspoon pepper)
- Handful pickled jalapenos + 1 Tablespoon brine
- Dollop soured cream

Directions

a) Combine cooked rice, chicken, salsa, black beans and spices in a bowl and spoon into the peppers.

b) Bake at 180°C for 20 minutes, then top with soured cream and extra jalapenos.

43. Italian Chicken Meatballs with Spaghetti

Serves: 4

Ingredients:

- 1 lb ground chicken breast
- 1 flax egg (1 tablespoon milled flax seed + 1 tablespoon water)
- 1 tablespoon chopped fresh basil
- 1 tablespoon chopped fresh Italian parsley
- ½ teaspoon dried oregano
- ¼ teaspoon onion powder
- ¼ teaspoon garlic powder

For the tomato sauce

- 2 (15oz) cans no-salt added tomato sauce
- ¾ cup California ripe black olives, sliced
- 1 tablespoon capers
- 1 teaspoon minced garlic
- 1 medium sweet onion, diced
- 1½ cups chopped button mushrooms

- ½ teaspoon black pepper
- ½ teaspoon dried thyme
- ½ teaspoon dried rosemary, crushed
- ⅓ teaspoon dried marjoram
- 1 tablespoon chopped fresh basil
- 1 tablespoon chopped fresh Italian parsley

For the spaghetti

- 4 large sweet potatoes (spiralized)

Directions:

For Chicken Meatballs:

a) Preheat the oven to 350°F.

b) Prepare you flax egg in a small bowl and set aside to gel.

c) In a large bowl, combine the ground chicken, herbs, spices, and flax egg. Mix well to combine.

d) Grease a large baking pan and form 12-14 meatballs, placing them evenly in the pan.

e) Bake for 30 minutes or until chicken is thoroughly cooked.

For Tomato Sauce:

f) Simply add all sauce **Ingredients** in a large soup pot and simmer for 10 minutes. Add the chicken meatballs and simmer for 5 more minutes.

For Spaghetti:

g) Simply spiralize your sweet potatoes (1 per person so 4 potatoes will be enough), using the C blade.

h) Add the spiralized potatoes in a microwave safe bowl with a few tablespoons of water and steam in the microwave for 3-5 minutes until slightly soft.

i) Serve meatballs and sauce over the spaghetti and enjoy!

44. Mediterranean Turkey Meatballs with Tzatziki

Serves: 50

Ingredients:

- 2 pounds ground turkey
- 2 tablespoons olive oil
- 1 medium onion, finely chopped
- Pinch of salt
- 1 medium zucchini, grated
- $1\frac{1}{2}$ tablespoons capers, chopped
- $\frac{1}{2}$ cup sun-dried tomatoes, chopped
- 2 slices whole wheat bread (or white bread)
- $\frac{1}{2}$ cup parsley
- 1 egg
- 1 large clove garlic, finely chopped
- $\frac{1}{2}$ teaspoon kosher salt
- $\frac{1}{2}$ teaspoon black pepper
- 1 tablespoon Worcestershire sauce
- $\frac{1}{2}$ cup shredded or grated parmesan cheese

- 2 tablespoons finely chopped fresh mint

For tzatziki sauce

- 8 ounces low-fat plain yogurt
- 1 large garlic clove, minced
- 1 lemon, zested
- 1 tablespoon fresh mint
- ½ cucumber, peeled

Directions:

a) Preheat oven to 375 degrees. Prepare two baking sheets by lining them with tin foil and spraying with vegetable spray.

b) Heat 1 tablespoon olive oil over medium high heat in a medium skillet. Add the onions and a pinch of salt and cook until translucent. Transfer onions to a large bowl.

c) Add the remaining tablespoon of olive oil to the skillet and add the grated zucchini. Sprinkle with a pinch of salt and cook until zucchini is wilted and softened – about 5 minutes. Transfer zucchini to the bowl with the onions. Add the capers and sun-dried tomatoes and stir to combine.

d) Place the bread in the bowl of a mini prep food processor and pulse until you have fine bread crumbs. Add the parsley and pulse several times until parsley is chopped and well combined with the bread crumbs. Transfer bread crumbs to the bowl. Add the egg, garlic, kosher salt, black pepper, Worcestershire sauce, parmesan cheese and mint to the bowl and stir.

e) Add the turkey meat and using your hands work the turkey into the binder until well combined. Scoop out a tablespoon of turkey mixture and roll it between your hands to form a meatball. Place the meatballs on the cookie sheet about 1 inch apart. Bake for 20-25 minutes until lightly browned and cooked through.

f) Meanwhile make the tzatziki sauce: Combine the garlic, lemon, mint and cucumber in a small bowl and stir the mixture. Add the yogurt and stir to combine. Cover and chill until ready to serve.

g) Transfer the meatballs to a platter and serve the tzatziki on the side.

45. Veggie and Beef Meatballs Marinara

Serves: 9

Ingredients:

- 6 teaspoons olive oil, divided
- 4 cloves garlic, sliced, divided
- 1 (28-ounce) can crushed tomatoes
- 1 teaspoon salt, divided
- 1 teaspoon sugar
- 1 teaspoon crushed red pepper flakes, divided, optional
- 1 small zucchini, roughly chopped
- 1 medium carrot, roughly chopped
- ½ small yellow onion, roughly chopped
- ¼ cup parsley leaves, plus more for garnishing
- 1 pound lean beef
- ½ cup oats
- ½ cup shredded parmesan, plus more for garnishing
- 1 large egg, beaten

Directions:

a) Preheat broiler on high. Make sure oven rack is about 4 inches below the heat source. Rub 1 teaspoon olive oil over the surface of a rimmed baking sheet.

b) In a large sauce pot, heat the remaining 5 teaspoons olive oil over medium heat. Add two cloves of garlic and cook until golden, about 3 minutes. Add tomatoes, $\frac{1}{2}$ teaspoon salt, sugar, and $\frac{1}{2}$ teaspoon red pepper flakes (if desired). Bring to a boil, reduce heat, and simmer, covered, for 10 minutes.

c) Meanwhile, in a food processor, combine zucchini, carrot, onion, remaining garlic, and parsley. Pulse until finely chopped. Transfer vegetable mixture to a large bowl. Add the beef, oats, parmesan, remaining salt, remaining red pepper flakes (if desired), and egg. Mix well.

d) Shape mixture into meatballs $1\frac{1}{2}$ inches in diameter. Arrange evenly on the prepared baking sheet. Broil until the tops of the meatballs are browned, about 5 minutes.

e) Gently transfer meatballs to the sauce pot and continue to cook, covered, for 10 minutes or until meatballs are cooked through. Remove from heat.

f) Serve as an appetizer or over cooked spaghetti as a main course. Garnish with additional parsley and parmesan if desired.

46. Honey Barbecue Chicken Meatballs

Serves: 4

Ingredients:

For the meatballs

- 1 lb. ground chicken
- 1 cup breadcrumbs
- ¼ cup thinly sliced green onions
- 2 large eggs, beaten
- 2 tablespoons minced fresh flat-leaf parsley
- 1 teaspoon minced garlic
- ½ teaspoon salt
- ¼ teaspoon ground black pepper

For the barbeque sauce

- 1 (8 oz.) can tomato sauce
- ¼ cup honey
- 1 tablespoon Worcestershire sauce
- 1 tablespoon red wine vinegar
- ½ teaspoon garlic powder

- ½ teaspoon salt
- ⅛ teaspoon ground black pepper

Directions:

a) Preheat oven to 400 degrees F. Line a baking sheet with aluminum foil and spray with cooking spray.

b) Prepare the meatballs. In a large bowl, add all of the meatball **Ingredients** and lightly mix together with your hands. Do not over-mix as this will produce tough meatballs.

c) Use your hands to roll out 12-14 golf ball-sized meatballs and spread them out on the baking sheet.

d) Bake for 15 minutes, or until meatballs are cooked through.

e) In the meantime, prepare the barbeque sauce. In a medium bowl, whisk all sauce **Ingredients** until well combined. Transfer the sauce to a large sauce pot. Turn the heat to medium-high and let cook for 7-8 minutes, stirring occasionally. The sauce will begin to thicken.

f) Reduce the heat to low. Add the cooked meatballs to the sauce and gently stir to coat the meatballs. Let the meatballs simmer in the sauce for 5 minutes, stirring occasionally.

47. Turkey Sweet Potato Meatballs

Serves: 16

Ingredients:

- 1 pound lean ground turkey
- 1 cup cooked, mashed sweet potato
- 1 egg
- 2 cloves garlic, minced
- 1 - 2 jalapenos, minced
- 1/2 cup almond meal (or breadcrumbs)
- 1/2 cup onion, diced
- 2 strips bacon, diced

Directions:

a) Combine all Ingredients in a large bowl.

b) Mix well and form into balls (I made about 16).

c) Bake at 400 degrees for 18-20 minutes (or until internal temp reaches 165 degrees), flipping once.

48. Easy Mexican Chickpea Salad

Serves 4.

Ingredients

- 19oz can chickpeas, rinsed and drained
- 1 large tomato, chopped
- 3 whole green onions, sliced OR S cup diced red onion
- 1/4 cup finely chopped cilantro (fresh coriander)
- 1 avocado, diced (optional)
- 2 Tablespoon vegetable or olive oil
- 1 Tablespoon lemon juice
- 1 teaspoon cumin
- 1/4 teaspoon chili powder
- 1/4 teaspoon salt

Directions

a) In a bowl, whisk the oil, lemon juice, cumin, chili powder, and salt.

b) Add chickpeas, tomatoes, onions, cilantro, and toss until combined.

c) If using avocado, add just before serving. Can be refrigerated for up to 2 days.

49. Tofu and Spinach Cannelloni

Serves 3-4

Ingredients

- 8 cannelloni/manicotti noodles (gluten free if required), cooked al dente
- 1 16 oz. jar of your favourite pasta sauce
- 2 Tablespoon olive oil
- 1 medium onion, chopped
- 1 1o oz. package of frozen spinach, thawed and chopped – or 1 bag of fresh baby spinach, chopped
- 16 oz. firm or silken tofu
- 1/2 cup soaked cashews, drained and finely ground (optional)
- 1/4 cup shredded carrots (optional)
- 2 Tablespoon lemon juice
- 1 clove garlic, minced
- 1 Tablespoon nutritional yeast
- 1 teaspoon salt
- 1/4 teaspoon black pepper
- Shredded vegan cheese, such as Daiya (optional)

Directions

a) In a nonstick skillet, saute the onions in the oil until translucent. Stir in the spinach and turn off the heat.

b) In a bowl, mix the tofu, cashews (if using), carrots, lemon juice, garlic, nutritional yeast, salt and pepper.

c) Add the spinach-onion mixture to the tofu mixture and stir until well-mixed.

d) Preheat oven to 350F. Pour a thin layer of pasta sauce on the bottom of a 9×133 pan.

e) Fill each cooked shell with filling using a small spoon. Line the filled shells up in the pan and cover with the rest of the pasta sauce.

f) Cover the pan with foil to keep the shells from drying out.

g) Bake for about 30 minutes, or until bubbling.

h) If adding vegan cheese, sprinkle it on top for the final 2 minutes in the oven.

50. Coconut Curry Lentil Soup

serves 4.

Ingredients

- 1 Tablespoon coconut oil (or olive oil)
- 1 large onion, chopped
- 2 cloves garlic, minced
- 1 Tablespoon fresh ginger, minced
- 2 Tablespoon tomato paste (or ketchup)
- 2 Tablespoon curry powder
- 1/2 teaspoon hot red pepper flakes
- 4 cups vegetable broth
- 1 400ml can coconut milk
- 1 400g can diced tomatoes
- 1. 5 cups dry red lentils
- 2-3 handfuls of chopped kale or spinach
- Salt and pepper, to taste
- Garnish: chopped cilantro (fresh coriander) and/or vegan sour cream

Directions

a) In a stockpot, heat the coconut oil over medium heat and stir-fry the onion, garlic and ginger until the onion is translucent, a couple minutes.

b) Add the tomato paste (or ketchup), curry powder, and red pepper flakes and cook for another minute.

c) Add the vegetable broth, coconut milk, diced tomatoes and lentils. Cover and bring to a boil, then simmer on low heat for 20-30 minutes, until the lentils are very tender. Season with salt and pepper.

d) {Make-Ahead: May be cooled, frozen in air-tight containers, and re-heated over medium-low heat.}

e) Before serving, stir in the kale/spinach and garnish with cilantro and/or vegan sour cream.

51. Indian Curry Quinoa

serves 4.

Ingredients

- 1 cup quinoa, rinsed and drained
- 1 can (400ml) coconut milk
- 1 can (400ml) diced tomatoes
- 3 Tablespoon curry powder
- 2 Tablespoon ketchup or tomato paste
- 2 Tablespoon coconut oil (or other vegetable oil)
- 1 large onion
- 1 clove garlic, minced
- 1 carrot, diced
- 1 can (400g) chickpeas, drained
- 2 large handfuls of chopped spinach or kale
- 1/2 teaspoon crushed red chili pepper salt and pepper cilantro (fresh coriander)

Directions

a) In a medium saucepan, mix quinoa, coconut milk, diced tomatoes (with juice), curry powder and ketchup/tomato paste, and bring to boil. Lower heat to lowest setting, cover saucepan and simmer until quinoa is ready, about 15 minutes.

b) While quinoa is cooking: in a frying pan, heat oil over medium heat and stir-fry the garlic and onion until translucent.

c) Add the carrot and saute for a couple minutes.

d) Add the chickpeas and cook for another couple minutes.

e) Add the spinach/kale and cook until wilted, about a minute.

f) Mix the veggies with the quinoa, season with salt, pepper and crushed red chili pepper, and garnish with cilantro before serving.

52. Grilled Vegetables on White Bean Mash

serves 2.

Ingredients

- 1 red pepper (capsicum), deseeded and quartered
- 1 aubergine (eggplant), sliced lengthways
- 2 courgettes (zucchinis), sliced lengthways
- 2 Tablespoon olive oil

For the Mash

- 410g can haricot beans, rinsed (I use Cannellini or White Kidney Beans)
- 1 garlic clove, crushed
- 100ml vegetable stock
- 1 Tablespoon chopped coriander (cilantro)
- Lemon wedges, to serve

Directions

a) Heat the grill. Arrange the vegetables over a grill pan and brush lightly with oil. Grill until lightly browned, turn them over, brush again with oil, then grill until tender.

b) Meanwhile, put the beans in a small pan with the garlic and stock. Bring to the boil, then simmer, uncovered, for 10 minutes.

c) Mash roughly with a potato masher, adding a little water or more stock if the mash seems too dry. Divide the veg and mash between 2 plates, drizzle over any leftover oil and sprinkle with black pepper and coriander. Add a lemon wedge to each plate and serve.

53. Oven roasted seitan

Ingredients:

- 1 cup of vital wheat gluten.
- 3 Tablespoon nutritional yeast.
- 1 teaspoon smoked paprika.
- 1 teaspoon dried thyme or 1 fresh spring thyme.
- 1 teaspoon dried rosemary.
- 1 Tablespoon garlic powder.
- 1 teaspoon sea salt.
- 1/4 teaspoon dried sage.
- 1 Tablespoon vegan Worcestershire sauce.
- 1 Tablespoon sugar complimentary BBQ Sauce.
- 2 Tablespoon liquid amino (or soy sauce).
- 1 cup Vegetable Broth.
- 4 cups of Vegetable Broth to simmer the seitan in.

DIRECTIONS:

a) Mix together your dry active ingredients in one bowl and your wet components in a second bowl.
b) Combine the wet with the dry and knead into a "dough".
c) Knead this dough for about 5 minutes or till the gluten is activated.

d) Bring about 4 cups of veggie broth to a simmer on medium-high.
e) The majority of dishes require you to wrap your seitan in plastic wrap prior to simmering, but that's only to keep the shape, and we discover that we like ours rustic and loaded with vegetable broth flavor.
f) Simply roll your seitan dough into a log and simmer in the covered pot of vegetable broth for 45 minutes.
g) After 45 minutes preheat your oven to 350° F and bake the seitan on a baking tray for 20 minutes, flipping it after 10 minutes.

54. Chickpea tofu

Ingredients for the chickpea tofu:

- 2 cups garbanzo bean flour.
- 1/4 cup dietary yeast.
- 2 teaspoon ground cumin.
- 1/2 teaspoon garlic powder.
- 1 teaspoon freshly ground black pepper.
- 1/4 teaspoon cayenne pepper.
- 1 Tablespoon coconut oil or olive oil.
- 1 1/2 teaspoon salt.

For the tahini sauce:

- 1/4 cup tahini.
- 1 clove garlic, minced.
- 1 teaspoon apple cider vinegar.
- Newly ground black pepper.
- 1 Tablespoon black sesame seeds.

Directions:

a) Preheat the oven to 400° F. in a big bowl, combine all the chickpea tofu components with 3/4 cup of water and mix well.

b) Line a baking pan with parchment paper, and gather the batter.

c) Bake for 20 minutes, or up until a toothpick inserted into the center comes out tidy.

d) Eliminate from the oven, let cool totally and cut into bite-size pieces.

e) In a separate bowl, mix together the tahini sauce active ingredients and 2 tablespoons of water (add more water if the tahini is too thick).

f) Serve the chickpea tofu on a bed of arugula, topped with the tahini sauce.

55. Braised tofu

Ingredients:

- 1 onion, cut into thin pieces.
- 1 14-ounce block firm tofu, cut into 16 squares.
- 1 tbs sugar.
- 1/2 -1 Tablespoon Korean chili powder.
- 3 Tablespoon soy sauce.
- 4 Tablespoon sake.
- 1 scallion, cut into thin slices.
- Toasted sesame seeds.

Directions:

a) Put onion slices on a non-stick skillet or frying pan, then leading with pieces of tofu.

b) Mix sugar, Korean chili powder, soy sauce, and sake together. Put over tofu slices.

c) Cover the frying pan with a lid. Turn the heat to high and cook until boiling. Turn the heat to medium-high, and cook for another 5 minutes, baste with the sauce a number of times.

d) Remove lid, turn the heat back to high, and cook till the sauce has actually minimized.

e) Shut off heat, transfer to a serving plate, garnish with scallions and sesame seeds. Serve immediately.

56. Spicy peanut butter tempeh

Ingredients:

- 22 oz tempeh, cut into 1-inch cubes.
- 6.5 oz wild rice, raw.
- Coconut oil spray.

Sauce:

- 4 Tablespoon peanut butter.
- 4 Tablespoon soy Sauce (low sodium).
- 4 Tablespoon coconut sugar.
- 2 Tablespoon red chili sauce.
- 2 teaspoon rice vinegar.
- 2 Tablespoon ginger.
- 3 cloves of garlic (or garlic paste).
- 6 Tablespoon water.

Cabbage:

- 5 oz purple cabbage, shaved/finely sliced.
- 1 lime, juice only.
- 2 teaspoon agave/apple bee-free honey.
- 3 teaspoon sesame oil.

- Garnish:
- Green onion, chopped.

Directions:

a) Mix all of the Ingredients for the spicy peanut sauce.

b) Cut the tempeh into 1-inch (2.5 cm) cubes.

c) Add sauce to the tempeh, stir, cover and marinade in the fridge for 2-3 hours or, preferably, overnight. Tempeh is actually good at soaking up the tastes of the marinade.

d) Preheat the oven to 375° F/190° C cook the rice as per packet directions.

e) Put the tempeh on a nonstick flat pan, spray with some coconut oil, bake in the oven for 25-30 minutes. Conserve any leftover marinade for serving.

f) Mix all of the components for the cabbage in a bowl and set aside to let it marinate.

57. Smoky chickpea tuna salad

Chickpea tuna:

- 15 oz. of cooked chickpeas canned or otherwise.
- 2-3 Tablespoon non-dairy plain yogurt or vegan mayo.
- 2 teaspoon Dijon mustard.
- 1/2 teaspoon ground cumin.
- 1/2 teaspoon smoked paprika.
- 1 Tablespoon fresh lemon juice.
- 1 celery stalk diced.
- 2 scallions chopped.
- Sea salt to taste.

Sandwich assembly:

- 4 pieces of rye bread or sprouted wheat bread.
- 1 cup infant spinach.
- 1 avocado sliced or cubed.
- Salt + pepper.

Directions:

a) In a food processor, pulse the chickpeas till they resemble a coarse, crumbly texture. Spoon the chickpeas into a medium-sized bowl and include the remainder of the active Ingredients, stirring till well combined. Season with plenty of sea salt to your own taste.

b) Layer the baby spinach on each slice of bread; add several heaping of chickpea tuna salad, spreading out evenly. Top with avocado slices, a couple of grains of sea salt, and newly ground pepper.

58. Thai quinoa salad

For the salad:

- 1/2 cup cooked quinoa
- 3 Tablespoon grated carrot.
- 2 Tablespoon red pepper, carefully sliced.
- 3 Tablespoon cucumber, finely sliced.
- 1/2 cup edamame
- 2 scallions, finely chopped.
- 1/4 cup red cabbage, finely sliced.
- 1 Tablespoon cilantro, carefully chopped.
- 2 Tablespoon roasted peanuts, chopped (optional).
- Salt.

Thai Peanut Dressing:

- 1 Tablespoon creamy natural peanut butter.
- 2 teaspoon low salt soy sauce.
- 1 teaspoon rice vinegar.
- 1/2 teaspoon sesame oil.
- 1/2 - 1 teaspoon sriracha sauce (optional).
- 1 Garlic clove, carefully minced.

- 1/2 teaspoon Grated Ginger.
- 1 teaspoon lemon juice.
- 1/2 teaspoon agave nectar (or honey).

Directions:

a) Combine all the Ingredients for the wearing a small bowl and blend till well combined.

b) Integrate quinoa with the veggies in a mixing bowl. Include the dressing and blend well to integrate.

c) Spray the roasted peanuts on the top and serve!

59. Turkish bean salad

For the salad:

- 1 1/2 cups boiled white beans.
- 1/2 cup chopped tomatoes.
- 1/2 cup sliced cucumber.
- 2 green peppers, sliced.
- 1/4 cup sliced parsley.
- 1/4 cup chopped fresh dill.
- 1/4 cup of sliced green onions.
- 4 tough boiled eggs.

Dressing

- 2 cups warm water.
- 2 red onions, thinly sliced.
- 1 Tablespoon lemon juice.
- 1 teaspoon vinegar.
- 1 teaspoon salt.
- 1 teaspoon sumac.

Directions:

a) In a large bowl, combine all components for the salad other than the eggs.

b) Whisk whatever for the dressing and put it over the salad. Provide it a good stir and top with sliced or halved eggs.

c) Throw sliced onions into really hot water, blanch for a minute, and transfer them into very cold water to stop cooking. Let them be in the cold water for a few minutes and drain well.

d) Mix lemon juice, salt, vinegar, and sumac and put this over drained onion. It's all set to utilize within 5 to 10 minutes. The longer it waits, the brighter the color it has.

e) Add red onions in the salad mixture and provide it an excellent stir. Leave some extra onions for the top.

f) Share the salad into bowls and leading with some more red onions.

60. Vegetable and quinoa bowls

Veggies:

- 4 medium whole carrots .
- 1 1/2 cups quartered infant yellow potatoes.
- 2 Tablespoon maple syrup.
- 2 Tablespoon olive oil.
- 1 healthy pinch each sea salt + black pepper.
- 1 Tablespoon sliced fresh rosemary.
- 2 cups halved Brussels sprouts.

Quinoa:

- 1 cup white quinoa well rinsed + drained.
- 1 3/4 cups water.
- 1 pinch sea salt.

Sauce:

- 1/2 cup tahini.
- 1 medium lemon, juiced (yields - 3 Tablespoon or 45 ml).
- 2-3 Tablespoon maple syrup.

For serving optional:

- Fresh herbs (parsley, thyme, and so on).

- Pomegranate arils.

Directions:

a) Preheat oven to 400 degrees F (204° C) and line a baking sheet with parchment paper

b) Include the carrots and potatoes to the sheet and drizzle with half of the maple syrup, half of the olive oil, the salt, pepper, and rosemary. Toss to integrate. Then bake for 12 minutes.

c) In the meantime, heat a pan over medium-high heat. Once hot, add rinsed quinoa to saute lightly before adding water to vaporize leftover wetness and highlight a nutty taste.

d) Prepare for 2-3 minutes, stirring often. Add water and a pinch of salt. Lastly, prepare dressing.

e) To serve, divide quinoa and veggies between serving bowls and leading with a generous drizzle of tahini sauce. Leading with garnish choices such as pomegranate arils or fresh herbs.

61. Almond butter tofu stir-fry

Ingredients

- 1 12-ounce package extra company tofu.
- 2 Tablespoon sesame oil (divided).
- 4 Tablespoon reduced-sodium tamari
- 3 Tablespoon maple syrup.
- 2 Tablespoon almond butter
- 2 Tablespoon lime juice.
- 1-2 teaspoon chili garlic sauce

Veggies

- Wild rice, white rice, or cauliflower rice.

Directions:

a) When the oven is preheated, unwrap tofu and cut into little cubes.

b) In the meantime, to a little blending bowl, add half of the sesame oil, tamari, maple syrup, almond butter, lime juice, and chili garlic sauce/red pepper flake/Thai chilies. Blend to integrate.

c) Include baked tofu to the almond butter-tamari sauce and let marinate for 5 minutes, stirring sometimes. The longer it marinates, the more extreme the flavor, however, I discover 5-10 minutes to be sufficient.

d) Heat a big frying pan over medium heat. When hot, add the tofu, leaving most of the marinade behind.

e) Cook for about 5 minutes, stirring sometimes, up until browned on all sides, and slightly caramelized. Get rid of from pan and set aside.

f) To the skillet, include remaining sesame oil of the marinade.

62. Quinoa chickpea buddha bowl

Chickpeas:

- 1 cup dry chickpeas.
- 1/2 teaspoon sea salt.

Quinoa:

- 1 Tablespoon olive, grapeseed, or avocado oil (or coconut).
- 1 cup white quinoa (well rinsed).
- 1 3/4 cup water.
- 1 healthy pinch sea salt.

Kale:

- 1 big package curly kale

Tahini sauce:

- 1/2 cup tahini.
- 1/4 teaspoon sea salt.
- 1/4 teaspoon garlic powder.
- 1/4 cup water.
- For serving:
- Fresh lemon juice.

Directions:

a) Either soak chickpeas overnight in cool water or use the quick-soak approach: Add rinsed chickpeas to a large pot and cover with 2 inches water. Drain, rinse, and include back to the pot.

b) To cook soaked chickpeas, add to a big pot and cover with 2 inches of water. Give a boil over high heat, then reduce heat to a simmer, include salt and stir, and cook uncovered for 40 minutes - 1 hour 20 minutes.

c) Sample a bean at the 40-minute mark to see how tender they are. You're looking for a simply tender bean with a little bit of bite, and the skins will begin to reveal indications of peeling. As soon as prepared, drain beans and set aside and sprinkle with a bit more salt.

d) Prepare dressing by including tahini, sea salt, and garlic powder to a little mixing bowl and whisking to integrate. Then add water a little at a time till it forms a pourable sauce.

e) Add 1/2 inch water to a medium pan and bring to a simmer over medium heat. Instantly remove the kale from the heat and transfer to a small dish for serving.

63. Seitan parmesan

Ingredients:

- 6 Tablespoon crucial wheat gluten.
- 1/2 teaspoon onion powder.
- 1/4 teaspoon poultry herbs.
- 1/4 teaspoon salt.
- 1 Tablespoon tahini.
- 5 Tablespoon vegan chicken broth.
- 1 vegan egg replacer.
- 6 Tablespoon flour.
- 1/4 teaspoon onion powder.
- 1/4 teaspoon garlic powder.
- 1/4 teaspoon salt.
- Pasta of option.
- Favorite pasta sauce.
- Vegan cheese, for serving.
- 1 big Brazil nut, for "Parmesan".

Directions:

a) Mix: 6 Tablespoon crucial wheat gluten, 1/2 teaspoon onion powder, 1/4 teaspoon poultry herbs, and 1/4 teaspoon salt.

b) Mix in a various bowl: 1 tablespoon tahini and 5 tablespoon vegan chicken broth or water.

c) Combined line 1 and 2 up until you have seitan dough. Knead dough for a minute.

d) Cover with water or broth. Once done, use a paper towel to push some extra water out of the patty.

e) Make a vegan egg as directed. Use a little extra water to make egg batter on the thinner side.

f) Make flour mix: 6 tablespoon flour, 1/4 onion powder, 1/4 garlic powder, and 1/4 salt.

g) Dip seitan patty into flour then vegan egg batter then flour once again. Fry on high/medium-high heat until golden brown.

h) Serve with pasta, sauce, and vegan cheese. Melt vegan cheese under "broil" setting, if wanted. Grate Brazil nut carefully for the Parmesan.

64. Red lentil patties

For the tomato sauce:

- 1 14-ounce can chopped tomatoes.
- A splash of agave syrup.
- 1 Tablespoon oil.
- 1 teaspoon red, white wine.
- Chili, dried herbs de provence, and paprika powder to taste.

For the lentil patties:

- 1 cup dry red lentils.
- 1 1/2 cups, plus 3 Tablespoon water.
- 1 teaspoon veggie broth powder.
- 1 teaspoon turmeric.
- 1 onion, diced.
- 1 clove of garlic, pressed.
- 1/2 teaspoon cumin.
- 1 flax egg.
- 2 Tablespoon of parsley.
- Salt and pepper, to taste.
- Oil, as needed.

To make the tomato sauce:

a) Add all active ingredients to a pot and give a boil. Minimize heat and simmer for about 30 minutes, stirring periodically. Get rid of from heat.

To make the lentil patties:

b) Combine lentils, water, vegetable broth, and turmeric in a pot and bring to a boil. If essential), reduce the heat and cook until the lentils are softened, and the water is absorbed (include more water. Stir periodically.

c) On the other hand, cook the onions in a frying pan.

d) Preheat oven to 390° F. line a baking sheet with baking paper and grease with oil.

e) In a bowl, integrate lentils, onions, garlic, cumin, flax egg, parsley, salt, and pepper. Mix well and let cool slightly.

f) Dampen hands with water, shape lentil patty, and put on baking paper. Brush with a bit of oil.

g) Bake the red lentil for about 20-25 minutes and serve with the tomato sauce.

65. Arugula pesto and zucchini

Ingredients:

- 2 slices of rye toast
- 1/2 of an avocado.
- 1/2 large zucchini.
- Bunch of watercress.
- 1 garlic clove.
- For arugula pesto:
- 2 big handfuls of arugula.
- 1 cup pine nuts (or any nut).
- 1 large handful of spinach.
- Juice of 1 lime.
- 1 teaspoon of sea salt.
- 3 Tablespoon olive oil.

Directions:

a) Start by making the arugula pesto by putting all the Ingredients into a food mill and whip up till the pesto becomes velvety and smooth.

b) Sauté the zucchini by first cutting it into very thin horizontal pieces. Warm the roughly sliced garlic clove, olive oil, sprinkle of sea salt, and a couple of splashes of water to a small pan on medium heat.

c) If the zucchini begins to dry out as it cooks, include the zucchini and sauté for 7 minutes - slowly include water.

d) Toast the bread, then spread out the pesto throughout the toast, add the zucchini and sliced avocado, and leading with watercress!

66. Vegetarian casserole

Ingredients:

- 1 Tablespoon olive or rapeseed oil.
- 1 onion, carefully sliced.
- 3 garlic cloves, sliced.
- 1 teaspoon smoked paprika.
- 1/2 teaspoon ground cumin.
- 1 Tablespoon dried thyme.
- 3 medium carrots, sliced.
- 2 medium sticks celery, finely sliced
- 1 red pepper, sliced.
- 1 yellow pepper, sliced.
- 2 x 400 g can of tomatoes or peeled cherry tomatoes.
- 1 vegetable stock cube made up to 250ml
- 2 courgettes, sliced thickly
- 2 sprigs fresh thyme.
- 250 g cooked lentils.

Directions:

a) Heat 1 Tablespoon olive or rapeseed oil in a huge, overwhelming based dish. Include 1 finely slashed onion and cook delicately for 5 – 10 minutes until mellowed.

b) Include 3 cut garlic cloves, 1 teaspoon smoked paprika, 1/2 teaspoon ground cumin, 1 Tablespoon dried thyme, 3 cut carrots, 2 finely cut celery sticks, 1 hacked red pepper and 1 cleaved yellow pepper and cook for 5 minutes.

c) Include two 400 g jars tomatoes, 250 ml vegetable stock (made with 1 stockpot), 2 thickly cut courgettes and 2 sprigs new thyme and cook for 20 - 25 minutes.

d) Take out the thyme sprigs. Mix in 250 g cooked lentils and take back to a stew. Present with wild and white basmati rice, squash or quinoa.

67. Roasted brussels sprouts

Ingredients:

- 1 lb Brussels sprouts, sliced in half.
- 1 shallot, chopped.
- 1 Tablespoon olive oil.
- Salt and pepper, to taste.
- 2 teaspoon balsamic vinegar.
- 1/4 cup pomegranate seeds.
- 1/4 cup goat cheese, crumbled.

Directions:

a) Preheat your oven to 400° F. Coat the Brussels sprouts with oil. Sprinkle with salt and pepper.

b) Transfer to a baking pan. Roast in the oven for 20 minutes.

c) Drizzle with the vinegar.

d) Sprinkle with the seeds and cheese before serving.

68. Avocado chickpea sandwich

Ingredients:

- 1 can no salt added chickpeas drained pipes and rinsed.
- 1 large ripe avocado.
- 1 1/2 Tablespoon lemon juice.
- 1/2 teaspoon hot chili pepper finely minced.
- Salt and pepper.
- 4 slices whole grain grew bread.
- 1 large treasure tomato sliced.
- 1/2 cup sweet microgreens.
- 1/2 cup shredded carrot.
- 1/2 cup prepared and shredded beet.

Directions:

a) In a bowl, mash the avocado up until relatively smooth, add in the lemon juice, hot chili pepper, and chickpeas. Season with salt and pepper.

b) To put together the sandwich, layer the slices of tomatoes on one slice of bread, add the microgreens, the beets, the chickpea salad, and the carrots. Enjoy!

69. Skillet quinoa

Ingredients:

- 1 cup sweet potato, cubed.
- 1/2 cup water.
- 1 Tablespoon olive oil.
- 1 onion, chopped.
- 3 cloves garlic, minced.
- 1 teaspoon ground cumin.
- 1 teaspoon ground coriander.
- 1/2 teaspoon chili powder.
- 1/2 teaspoon dried oregano.
- 15 oz black beans, rinsed and drained.
- 15 oz roasted tomatoes.
- 1 1/4 cups vegetable broth.
- 1 cup frozen corn 1 cup quinoa (uncooked).
- Salt to taste.
- 1/2 cup light sour cream.
- 1/2 cup fresh cilantro leaves.

Directions:

a) Add the water and sweet potato in a pan over medium heat. Bring to a boil.

b) Reduce heat and cook until sweet potato is tender.

c) Add the oil and onion.

d) Cook for 3 minutes. Stir in the garlic and spices and cook for 1 minute.

e) Add the rest of the Ingredients except the sour cream and cilantro. Cook for 20 minutes.

f) Serve with sour cream and top with the cilantro before serving.

70. Sticky tofu with noodles

Ingredients:

- 1/2 big cucumber.
- 100 ml rice red wine vinegar.
- 2 Tablespoon golden caster sugar.
- 100 ml veggie oil.
- 200 g pack company tofu, cut into 3cm cubes.
- 2 Tablespoon maple syrup.
- 4 Tablespoon brown or white miso paste.
- 30 g white sesame seeds.
- 250 g dried soba noodles.
- 2 spring onions, shredded, to serve.

Directions:

a) Using a peeler, cut thin ribbons off the cucumber, leaving the seeds behind. Put the ribbons in a bowl and set aside. Gently heat the vinegar, sugar, 1/4 teaspoon salt, and 100ml water in a pan over medium heat for 3-5 minutes up until the sugar liquefies, then pour over the cucumbers and leave to pickle in the fridge while you prepare the tofu.

b) Heat all but 1 Tablespoon of the oil in a large, non-stick frying pan over medium heat up until bubbles begin to rise to the surface. Include the tofu and fry for 7-10 minutes.

c) In a little bowl, blend together the honey and miso. Spread the sesame seeds out on a plate. Brush the fried tofu with the sticky honey sauce and set aside any leftovers. Coat the tofu evenly in the seeds, sprinkle with a little salt and leave in a warm place.

d) Prepare the noodles and toss with the rest of the oil, the remaining sauce and 1 Tablespoon of the cucumber pickling liquid. Cook for 3 minutes up until warmed through.

71. Vegan BBQ teriyaki tofu

Ingredients:

- 4 Tablespoon low-salt soy sauce.
- 2 Tablespoon soft brown sugar.
- Pinch ground ginger.
- 2 Tablespoon mirin.
- 3 teaspoon sesame oil.
- 350 g block extremely firm tofu (see tip below) cut into thick slices.
- 1/2 Tablespoon rapeseed oil.
- 2 courgettes, sliced horizontally into strips.
- 200 g tender stem broccoli.
- White and black sesame seeds, to serve.

Directions:

a) Mix the soy sauce, soft brown sugar, ginger and mirin with 1 teaspoon sesame oil and brush it all over the pieces of tofu. Put them in a large, shallow meal and put over any remaining marinade. Chill for at least 1 hr.

b) Heat the barbecue till the coals are glowing white, or heat a griddle pan. Mix the staying sesame oil with the rapeseed oil and brush the courgette slices and broccoli. Barbecue (or griddle) them over the coals for 7-10 minutes or till they hurt and then reserved and keep warm.

c) Barbecue the tofu pieces on both sides over the coals for 5 minutes (or use the frying pan) up until they turn brown and go crisp at the edges. Serve the tofu on a bed of the veg with the staying marinade and scatter over the sesame seeds.

72. Sprouts with green beans

Ingredients:

- 600 g brussels sprouts, quartered and cut.
- 600 g green beans.
- 1 Tablespoon olive oil.
- Zest and juice 1 lemon.
- 4 Tablespoon toasted pine nuts.

Directions:

a) Cook for a couple of seconds, then add the vegetables and stir-fry for 3-4 minutes up until the sprouts color a little.

b) Add a squeeze of lemon juice and salt and pepper to taste.

73. Crusted tofu with radish

Ingredients:

- 200 g firm tofu.
- 2 Tablespoon sesame seeds.
- 1 Tablespoon Japanese shichimi togarashi.
- Spice mix.
- 1/2 Tablespoon corn flour.
- 1 Tablespoon sesame oil.
- 1 Tablespoon veggie oil.
- 200 g tender stem broccoli.
- 100 g sugar snap peas.
- 4 radishes, very finely sliced.
- 2 spring onions, carefully sliced.
- 3 kumquats, very finely sliced.
- For the dressing
- 2 Tablespoon low-salt Japanese soy sauce.
- 2 Tablespoon yuzu juice (or 1 Tablespoon each lime and grapefruit juice).
- 1 teaspoon golden caster sugar.

- 1 small shallot, finely diced.
- 1 teaspoon grated ginger.

Directions:

a) Slice the tofu in half, cover well in kitchen paper and place on a plate. Put a heavy fry pan on top to squeeze the water out of it.

b) Mix together the sesame seeds, Japanese spice mix and corn flour in a bowl. Spray over the tofu until well layered. Set aside.

c) In a little bowl, mix the dressing Ingredients together. Bring a pan of water to the boil for the vegetables and heat the two oils in a big frying pan.

d) When the fry-pan is very hot, include the tofu and fry for 1 minute approximately on each side up until nicely browned.

e) When the water is boiling, prepare the broccoli and sugar snap peas for 2-3 minutes.

74. Lentil lasagna

Ingredients:

- 1 Tablespoon olive oil.
- 1 onion, chopped.
- 1 carrot, sliced.
- 1 celery stick, chopped.
- 1 garlic clove, squashed.
- 2 x 400 g cans lentils, drained, rinsed.
- 1 Tablespoon corn flour.
- 400 g can chopped tomato.
- 1 teaspoon mushroom ketchup.
- 1 teaspoon sliced oregano (or 1 teaspoon dried).
- 1 teaspoon veggie stock powder.
- 2 cauliflower heads, broken into florets.
- 2 Tablespoon unsweetened soya milk.
- Pinch of newly grated nutmeg.
- 9 dried egg-free lasagna sheets.

Directions:

a) Heat the oil in a pan, add the carrot, celery and onion, and carefully prepare for 10-15 minutes until soft. Add the garlic, cook for a couple of minutes, then stir in the lentils and corn flour.

b) Add the tomatoes plus a can full of water, the mushroom catsup, oregano, stock powder and some seasoning. Simmer for 15 minutes, stirring occasionally.

c) Cook the cauliflower in a pan of boiling water for 10 minutes or until tender. Drain pipes, then purée with the soya milk using a hand blender or food mill. Season well and include the nutmeg.

d) Include another 3rd of the lentil mix, then spread out a third of the cauliflower purée on top, followed by a layer of pasta. Top with the last third of lentils and lasagna, followed by the remaining purée.

e) Cover loosely with foil and bake for 35-45 minutes, eliminating the foil for the final 10 minutes of cooking.

75. Lentil meatballs

For the meatballs:

- 3/4 cup dried brown and green or French lentils.
- 1 1/2 cups low-sodium vegetable broth - or chicken broth, plus extra as needed.
- 2 teaspoon olive oil.
- 1/2 cup diced yellow onion - about 1/2 medium onion.
- 1 cup shredded carrots.
- 2 cloves garlic - minced (about 2 teaspoons).
- 1/2 cup old-fashioned rolled oats-- or quick - cooking oats, do not utilize immediate or steel-cut.
- 1/4 cup chopped fresh Italian parsley.
- 1 1/2 Tablespoon tomato paste.
- 1 teaspoon dried oregano.
- 1/2 teaspoon kosher salt.
- 1/4 teaspoon black pepper.
- 1 big egg.

a) Prepare entire wheat pasta noodles zucchini noodles, or sweet potato noodles..

b) Add the rinsed lentils to a medium saucepan with the veggie broth.

c) Cook Onions, Garlic and carrots in oil.

d) Pulse oats and parsley a few times to begin breaking up the oats. Add the prepared lentils, onion mix, tomato paste, oregano, salt, and pepper then crack in the egg. Pulse a few more times till the mix is integrated but the lentils still have some texture.

e) Roll the lentil mix into balls that are roughly 1 1/2 inches across, about the size of a golf ball. Cook for 10 minutes.

76. Hazelnut-crusted pork medallions

Ingredients

- 10 ounces pork tenderloin, sliced into $\frac{1}{2}$-inch thick rounds
- 1 teaspoon dijon mustard
- $\frac{1}{2}$ cup finely chopped hazelnuts
- 2 tablespoons chopped fresh basil
- Salt and freshly milled black pepper to taste
- 2 tablespoons olive oil
- 1 cup low-sodium chicken broth
- $\frac{1}{4}$ cup half-and-half cream
- 1 cup sliced beets, drained

a) With a mallet or meat pounder, pound each pork round between sheets of wax paper until $\frac{1}{4}$ inch thickness. Mix the mustard, hazelnuts, basil, and salt and pepper in a bowl.

b) Dredge the pork medallions in the mustard mixture and set it aside. Heat a dry skillet for 2 minutes, then add the oil and heat over medium-high heat for 1 minute. Add the dredged pork medallions and sauté for 30 seconds to 1 minute per side, until the nuts are lightly browned (the pork will finish cooking in the sauce).

c) Remove the medallions from the pan and keep warm. Add the broth to the pan and deglaze, scraping up all of the brown bits that stick to the bottom. Stir in the cream and simmer for 3 more minutes. Return the medallions to the sauce and cook for 2 more minutes.

d) Arrange the beet slices on two plates. Place each medallion over a beet slice and serve at once.

77. Pork chops with relish

RELISH

- ¼ cup chopped plum tomatoes
- ¼ cup chopped red onion
- 2 tablespoons red wine vinegar
- 2 tablespoons extra-virgin olive oil
- 1 garlic clove, chopped
- 2 tablespoons chopped fresh basil
- 1 teaspoon dried oregano
- ½ teaspoon salt
- Freshly milled black pepper to taste

MARINADE

- 2 tablespoons red wine vinegar
- 2 tablespoons olive oil
- 1 garlic clove, chopped
- Two 10-ounce thick-cut pork chops
- Salt and freshly milled black pepper to taste
- 2 tablespoons vegetable oil chopped fresh flat-leaf parsley
- Fresh parmesan cheese curls for garnish

a) Toss the relish Ingredients together in a small bowl. Set it aside.

b) Whisk marinade mixture in a shallow baking dish. Place the pork chops in the marinade, turning to coat both sides, and set aside for 10 minutes. Now remove the chops from the marinade and drain off the excess. Salt and pepper the chops generously.

c) Preheat a dry cast-iron skillet for 3 minutes over high heat. Add the vegetable oil and heat for 1 more minute. Place the chops in the hot oil and cook to medium-rare, 3 to 4 minutes per side, or to desired degree of doneness.

d) Place the chops on a plate, top with relish, chopped parsley, and Parmesan cheese curls. Serve at once.

78. Pork with spaghetti squash

Ingredients

- 1 teaspoon olive oil
- 12 ounces pork tenderloin, cut into 1-inch-thick medallions
- $\frac{1}{2}$ teaspoon kosher salt
- $\frac{1}{4}$ teaspoon freshly milled black pepper
- 1 tablespoon minced shallots
- 1 cup dry red wine
- $\frac{1}{4}$ teaspoon cornstarch
- Grated zest from $\frac{1}{2}$ lemon plus 2 teaspoons fresh lemon juice
- 1 tablespoon all-fruit (no sugar added) red currant jelly
- 1 teaspoon Dijon mustard
- 2 cups Roasted Spaghetti Squash

a) Heat a large skillet over medium-high heat, then film it with the oil. Meanwhile, dry the pork pieces on paper towels, and season with salt and pepper. Sauté until crisp and brown on the outside, and no longer pink in the middle, 3 to 4 minutes per side. Transfer to warmed dinner plates and reserve.

b) Add the shallots to the pan and cook about 30 seconds. Add the wine, bring to a boil, and reduce to about $\frac{1}{4}$ cup, 5 minutes or so. Dissolve the cornstarch in the lemon juice and whisk it into the sauce. Cook, stirring, until the sauce is thick and satiny-looking. Remove from the heat and stir in the jelly and mustard. Taste and adjust seasonings with salt and pepper.

c) To serve, make a nest of Roasted Spaghetti Squash on each plate and top with pork medallions and sauce.

79. Spicy quinoa falafel

Ingredients:

- 1 Cup cooked quinoa.
- 1 Can garbanzo beans.
- Half of a small red onion.
- 1 Tablespoon Tahini.
- 2 teaspoon cumin powder.
- 1 teaspoon coriander powder.
- 1/4 cup chopped parsley.
- 3 garlic cloves.
- Juice of half a lemon.
- 1 Tablespoon coconut oil.
- 1 Tablespoon tamari (GF soy sauce).
- 1/2 - 1 teaspoon chili flakes.
- Sea salt preparation.

Directions:

a) Toss the garbanzo beans, red onion, garlic, tahini, chili flakes, cumin, coriander, lemon juice, and salt into a food mill and pulse on-and-off for 15 seconds so that it breaks down the beans, however, doesn't puree them.

b) Roll the mixture with your hands into little balls (about 2 tablespoons of dough for each) and Put on a baking sheet.

c) Put them in the fridge for 1 hour.

d) Sprinkle with a little flour on both sides.

e) Heat coconut oil in a large pan on medium heat.

f) Add the falafel balls and cook 3-5 minutes on each side.

80. Butternut squash galette

Ingredients:

- 1 1/2 cups spelt flour.
- 6-8 sage leaves.
- 1/4 cups cold water.
- 6 Tablespoon coconut oil.
- Sea salt.
- For the filling:
- 1 Tablespoon olive oil.
- 1/4 red onion, thinly sliced.
- 1 Tablespoon sage leaves.
- 1/2 red apple, very finely sliced.
- 1/4 butternut squash, skin removed and very finely sliced.
- 1 Tablespoon coconut oil, divided and booked for topping.
- 2 Tablespoon sage, reserved for topping.
- Sea salt.

Directions:

a) Preheat your oven to 350° F.

b) Make the crust by adding the flour, sea salt and sage leaves into the food mill. Gradually include the coconut oil and water, and pulse regularly as this gently blends into the flour. Pulse only enough up until the components integrate together, 30 seconds or so.

c) In the meantime, make the filling. In a small pan on medium-high heat, warm the olive oil. Include in the onions, pinch of salt, one teaspoon of sage leaves, and sauté for about 5 minutes. Set this aside as you roll out your dough into a circle, about 1/4 inch thick.

d) Mix the squash and apples in a little bowl with a drizzle of olive oil and sea salt. Add the butternut squash and apple slices on top of the onions (simply as you see it in the image).

e) Gently fold the edges of the crust on top of the outer sides of the squash.

f) Include small chunks of the coconut oil on top of the galette, together with the sage leaves, and bake in the oven for 20-25 minutes, or until the crust is flaky and the squash is cooked through.

81. Quinoa with curry paste

Ingredients

- 2 Tablespoon of the stem of the fresh cilantro.
- 2 little handfuls of fresh cilantro leaves.
- 6 cloves of garlic.
- 1 Tablespoon powdered coriander.
- 1/2 Tablespoon powdered cumin.
- 1-inch nob of ginger (without its skin).
- Juice of 1 lime.
- 1 lemongrass stalk
- 1/2 cup shallots or white onion.
- 1 teaspoon chili flakes.
- Sea salt.
- green curry

Directions:

a) Start by making the curry paste by just mixing everything into the food mill up until it's well blended and ground down into a paste.

b) Now for the curry - on medium/high heat warm the coconut oil and onions for 5 minutes. Include all the vegetables, coconut sugar, curry paste and 1/4 cup water and let this simmer with the cover on for about 10 minutes.

c) Add more water gradually so that the veggies do not burn. As soon as the veggies have cooked down, include the coconut milk and 1 cup water, and cook for another 10 minutes up until the veggies are completely cooked. Stir in the fresh lime juice, additional cilantro leaves and, leading over brown rice or quinoa!

82. Baked smoky carrot bacon

Ingredients:

- 3 large carrots.
- 2 Tablespoon rapeseed oil.
- 1 teaspoon garlic powder.
- 1 teaspoon smoked paprika.
- 1 teaspoon salt.

Directions:

a) Wash carrot (no requirement to peel) and piece, lengthwise, using a mandolin. Lay the carrot strips on a baking sheet lined with parchment paper. Preheat oven to 320° F. stir together staying components in a small bowl and then brush carrot strips on both sides.

b) Put in the oven for 15 minutes, or when the carrot strips are wavy.

83. Salmon over spaghetti squash

Ingredients

- ½ teaspoon five-spice powder
- 1 teaspoon grated orange zest
- ½ teaspoon sugar
- ¼ teaspoon kosher salt
- ½ teaspoon freshly milled black pepper
- Two 6-ounce salmon fillets
- 2 teaspoons Dijon mustard
- 1 tablespoon peanut oil
- 2 cups Roasted Spaghetti Squash
- 2 tablespoons minced fresh cilantro

a) Stir together the five-spice powder with orange zest, sugar, salt, and pepper in a small bowl. Rub into both sides of the fillets on wax paper. Brush the mustard onto the fillets.

b) Heat a large skillet over medium-high heat, then film the bottom with the oil. Pan-fry the fillets, turning only once, until crisp and brown on the outside, 5 to 8 minutes total.

c) Meanwhile, divide the squash between two warmed dinner plates. Top with the fish fillets and garnish with the cilantro.

84. Poached salmon on leeks

Ingredients

- 4 cups (two 15½-ounce cans) low-sodium chicken broth
- 1 cup water
- 3 tablespoons herbes de Provence
- 1 medium leek, quartered and cleaned (see note)
- Two 6-ounce salmon fillets
- 2 tablespoons unsalted butter ¼ cup heavy cream

a) In a large skillet with a tight-fitting lid, combine the chicken broth, water, and the herbes de Provence. Bring to a boil over high heat, cover, then reduce the heat to medium-low. Add the leeks and cook for 7 to 10 minutes.

b) Place the salmon fillets on top of the leeks, skin side down, cover and cook for 4 to 5 minutes, or until the salmon is opaque. Using a slotted spoon or tongs, remove the salmon and leeks to a warm plate and cover. Add butter and cream to the pan and cook for 5 minutes reducing the sauce.

c) Divide the sauce between two soup plates. Top with leeks, then salmon. Serve immediately.

85. Grilled swordfish with salsa

Ingredients

- Two 6-ounce boneless, skinless swordfish steaks, $\frac{3}{4}$ inch thick
- 1 tablespoon olive oil
- 2 cups shredded iceberg lettuce
- 1 cup sliced radishes
- 1 Hass avocado
- 2 tablespoons best-quality salsa pumped up with a little fresh cilantro
- Grated zest and juice of 1 lime

a) Preheat the gas, charcoal, or electric grill. Brush the fish with olive oil on both sides. Grill the fish, turning once after it has browned on the bottom (about 2 minutes), then finish on the second side, cooking until the fish is translucent in the middle (2 to 3 more minutes).

b) Meanwhile, make a bed of lettuce, radishes, and avocado on two warmed dinner plates. Transfer the cooked fish to the dinner plates and top each steak with a big dollop of salsa. Squeeze lime juice over all and sprinkle with zest.

86. Tuna steaks with mayo

Ingredients

- 2 teaspoons mayonnaise
- 2 tablespoons minced fresh or 2 teaspoons dried tarragon plus tarragon sprigs for garnish
- Two 6-ounce tuna steaks, 1 inch thick
- Salt and cracked pepper to taste
- 1 teaspoon olive oil
- Squashed Winter Squash

a) Stir together the mayo and tarragon in a small bowl. Cover and set aside. Heat a heavy skillet or ridged grill pan over medium-high heat. Pat the tuna dry with paper towels, then season to taste with salt and cracked pepper.

b) Dab olive oil over the surfaces of the fish. Pan grill about 3 minutes per side for medium. Transfer to warmed dinner plates. Top each steak with a dollop of tarragon mayonnaise, and garnish with tarragon sprigs. Place a mound of squash beside the tuna.

87. Squashed winter squash

Ingredients

- One $\frac{1}{2}$-pound winter squash (butternut, hubbard)
- 2 tablespoons unsalted butter
- Salt and freshly milled black pepper to taste

a) Prick the surface of the squash in several places with a fork. Place it in the microwave, and cook on high until it's soft through, about 8 minutes.

88. Skewered scallops prosciutto

Ingredients

- 2 ounces thinly sliced prosciutto
- 12 large fresh basil leaves
- 12 ounces large sea scallops

CREAMED SPINACH

- 1 tablespoon olive oil
- 12 ounces fresh baby spinach
- 2 tablespoons cream
- Salt to taste
- ½ teaspoon freshly milled black pepper
- Pinch of freshly grated nutmeg

a) Soak 12 small wooden skewers in water for at least 20 minutes. Place a prosciutto slice on a work surface, then lay a basil leaf at one end. Top with a scallop. Wrap the prosciutto around the scallop and basil, tucking in the sides. Repeat the process to make 12 packets. Thread onto the soaked skewers, cover, and set them aside. Heat a grill or a large skillet.

b) Grill the packets over a medium charcoal fire or in the skillet, filmed with some of the olive oil, until the prosciutto begins to sizzle. Turn once and continue cooking, no more than 5 minutes total.

c) Meanwhile, sauté spinach in a large skillet with a little of the oil, just until wilted. Add the cream, season to taste with salt, pepper, and a little nutmeg. To serve, make a bed of creamed spinach on each of two warmed dinner plates. Slide the scallop packet off the skewers and arrange them on the spinach.

89. Seitan and black bean

For the sauce:

- 400 g can black beans, drained pipes, and washed.
- 75 g dark brown soft sugar.
- 3 garlic cloves.
- 2 Tablespoon soy sauce.
- 1 teaspoon Chinese five-spice powder.
- 2 Tablespoon rice vinegar.
- 1 Tablespoon smooth peanut butter.
- 1 red chili, finely chopped.

For the stir-fry:

- 350 g jar marinade seitan pieces.
- 1 Tablespoon corn flour.
- 2-3 Tablespoon vegetable oil.
- 1 red pepper, sliced.
- 300 g pak choi, sliced.
- 2 spring onions, sliced.
- Prepared rice noodles or rice, to serve.

Directions:

a) Start by making the sauce, idea half the beans into the bowl of a food mill with the remainder of the active Ingredients, and add 50ml water. Season, then blend until smooth. Put into a pan and heat carefully for about 5 minutes or up until glossy and thick.

b) Drain pipes the seitan and pat dry with cooking area paper. Toss the seitan pieces in a bowl with the corn flour and reserved. Heat your wok to a high temperature level, include a little oil, then the seitan - you may require to do this in batches. Stir-fry for around 5 minutes until golden brown at the edges. Eliminate the seitan from the wok using a slotted spoon and set aside on a plate.

c) If the wok is dry at this stage, add 1 teaspoon veggie oil. Prepare for 3-4 minutes, then return the seitan to the pan, stir in the sauce, and bring to the boil for 1 min.

90. Curried tofu covers

Ingredients:

- 1/2 red cabbage, shredded.
- 4 loaded Tablespoon dairy-free yogurt
- 3 Tablespoon mint sauce.
- 3 x 200 g packs tofu, each cut into 15 cubes.
- 2 Tablespoon tandoori curry paste.
- 2 Tablespoon oil.
- 2 onions, sliced.
- 2 large garlic cloves, sliced.
- 8 chapattis.
- 2 limes, cut into quarters.

Directions:

a) Mix the cabbage, yogurt and mint sauce, season and reserved. Toss the tofu with the tandoori paste and 1 tablespoon of the oil. Heat a frying pan and cook the tofu, in batches, for a few minutes each side till golden. Eliminate from the pan with a slotted spoon and.

b) Add the staying oil to the pan, stir in the onions and garlic, and cook for 8-10 minutes till softened. Return the tofu to the pan and season well.

c) Warm the chapattis following pack directions, then leading every one with some cabbage, followed by the curried tofu and a great squeeze of lime.

91. Thai salad with tempeh

Salad:

- 6 ounces vermicelli noodles
- 2 medium whole carrots, "ribboned" with a vegetable peeler or spiralizer.
- 2 stalks green onions
- 1/4 cup sliced cilantro.
- 2-3 Tablespoon sliced mint.
- 1 cup loosely packed spinach
- 1 cup very finely sliced red cabbage.
- 1 medium red bell pepper.
- 1 batch marinated peanut tempeh.

Dressing:

- 1/3 cup salted velvety peanut butter, almond butter, or sun butter.
- 3 Tablespoon gluten-free tamari.
- 3 Tablespoon maple syrup.
- 1 teaspoon chili garlic sauce
- 1 medium lime, juiced (yields - 3 Tablespoon or 45 ml).
- 1/4 cup water (to thin).

Directions:

a) Cook rice noodles according to package guidelines, rinse, drain, and reserved to cool.

b) To a large serving bowl, add cooked and cooled noodles, carrots, green onions, cilantro, mint, spinach, cabbage, and red bell pepper and toss loosely to integrate. Reserve.

c) Make dressing.

d) Include 1/2 of the tempeh (optional) and 1/2 of the sauce to the salad and toss. Leading with remaining tempeh and sauce. Serve immediately.

92. Puffed quinoa bar

Ingredients:

- 3 Tablespoon coconut oil.
- 1/2 cup raw cacao powder.
- 1/3 cup maple syrup.
- 1 Tablespoon tahini
- 1 teaspoon cinnamon.
- 1 teaspoon vanilla powder.
- Sea salt.

Directions:

a) In a small pan over medium-low heat, melt the coconut oil, raw cacao, tahini, cinnamon, maple sea, syrup, and vanilla salt together till it ends up being a thicker chocolate mixture.

b) Put the chocolate sauce over the popped quinoa and mix well. Scoop a large tablespoon of the chocolate crispies into little baking cups.

c) Pop them in the freezer for a minimum of 20 minutes to harden. Store in the freezer and delight in!

93. Chocolate chunk cookies

Ingredients:

- 2 cups all-purpose gluten-free flour.
- 1 teaspoon baking soda.
- 1 teaspoon sea salt.
- 1/4 cup vegan yogurt.
- 7 Tablespoon vegan butter.
- 3 Tablespoon cashew butter
- 1 1/4 cup coconut sugar.
- 2 chia eggs.
- Dark chocolate bar, burglarize portions.

Directions:

a) Preheat the oven to 375° F

b) In a medium-size mixing bowl, blend gluten-free flour, salt and baking soda. Set aside while you melt the butter.

c) Include the butter, yogurt, cashew butter, coconut sugar into a bowl and using a mixing stand or hand mixer, blend for a few minutes up until combined.

d) Include the chia eggs and mix well.

e) Include the flour to chia egg mix and blend on low up until integrated.

f) Fold in the chocolate chunks.

g) Place the dough in the refrigerator to set for 30 minutes.

h) Eliminate the dough from the refrigerator and let it come down to room temperature, about 10 minutes, and line a cookie sheet with parchment paper.

i) Using your hands, scoop 1 1/2 tablespoon size of cookie dough onto the parchment paper. Leave a little room in-between each cookie.

j) Bake cookies for 9-11 minutes. Delight in!

94. Shelled edamame dip

Ingredients:

- 1/2 cup sliced red onion.
- Juice of 1 lime.
- Sea salt.
- A handful of cilantro.
- Diced tomatoes (optional).
- Chili flakes.

Directions:

a) Just pulse the onion in a blender for a few seconds. Then add the remainder of the active ingredients and pulse until the edamame is blended into big portions.

b) Take pleasure in as a spread on toast, for a sandwich, as a dip or as a pesto sauce!

95. Matcha cashew cups

Ingredients:

- 2/3 cup cacao butter.
- 3/4 cup cacao powder.
- 1/3 cup maple syrup.
- 1/2 cup cashew butter, or any you'd like.
- 2 teaspoon matcha powder.
- Sea salt.

Directions:

a) Fill a little pan with 1/3 cup of water and location a bowl on top, covering the pan. Once the bowl is hot, and the water below is boiling melt the cacao butter inside the bowl, turn on the heat and. Once it has melted, remove from heat, and stir in the maple syrup and cacao powder for a couple of minutes till the chocolate thickens.

b) Using a medium-size cupcake holder fill the bottom layer with a generous tablespoon of the chocolate mixture. Pop them into the freezer for 15 minutes to set.

c) Take the frozen chocolate out of the freezer and dollop 1 tablespoon size of the matcha/cashew butter dough on top of the frozen chocolate layer. Sprinkle with sea salt and let this sit in the freezer for 15 minutes.

96. Chickpea choco slices

Ingredients:

- 400 g can chickpeas, rinsed, drained.
- 250 g almond butter.
- 70 ml maple syrup.
- 15 ml vanilla paste.
- 1 pinch salt.
- 2 g baking powder.
- 2 g baking soda.
- 40 g vegan chocolate chips.

Directions:

a) Preheat oven to 180° C/350° F.

b) Grease large baking pan with coconut oil.

c) Combine chickpeas, almond butter, maple syrup, vanilla, salt, baking powder, and baking soda in a food blender.

d) Blend until smooth. Stir in half the chocolate chips spread the batter into the prepared baking pan.

e) Sprinkle with reserved chocolate chips.

f) Bake for 45-50 minutes or until an inserted toothpick comes out clean.

97. Sweet green cookies

Ingredients:

- 165 g green peas.
- 80 g chopped medjool dates.
- 60 g silken tofu, mashed.
- 100 g almond flour.
- 1 teaspoon baking powder.
- 12 almonds.

Directions:

a) Preheat oven to 180° C/350° F.

b) Combine peas and dates in a food processor.

c) Process until the thick paste is formed.

d) Transfer the pea mixture into a bowl. Stir in tofu, almond flour, and baking powder. Shape the mixture into 12 balls.

e) Arrange balls onto baking sheet, lined with parchment paper. Flatten each ball with oiled palm.

f) Insert an almond into each cookie. Bake the cookies for 25-30 minutes or until gently golden.

g) Cool on a wire rack before serving.

98. Banana bars

Ingredients:

- 130 g smooth peanut butter.
- 60 ml maple syrup.
- 1 banana, mashed.
- 45 ml water.
- 15 g ground flax seeds.
- 95 g cooked quinoa.
- 25 g chia seeds.
- 5 ml vanilla.
- 90 g quick cooking oats.
- 55 g whole-wheat flour.
- 5 g baking powder.
- 5 g cinnamon.
- 1 pinch salt.
- Topping:
- 5 ml melted coconut oil.
- 30 g vegan chocolate, chopped.

Directions:

a) Preheat oven to 180° C/350° F.

b) Line 16cm baking dish with parchment paper.

c) Combine flax seeds and water in a small bowl. Place aside 10 minutes.

d) In a separate bowl, combine peanut butter, maple syrup, and banana. Fold in the flax seeds mixture.

e) Once you have a smooth mixture, stir in quinoa, chia seeds, vanilla extract, oat, whole-wheat flour, baking powder, cinnamon, and salt.

f) Pour the batter into prepared baking dish. Cut into 8 bars.

g) Bake the bars for 30 minutes.

h) In the meantime, make the topping; combine chocolate and coconut oil in a heatproof bowl. Set over simmering water, until melted.

i) Remove the bars from the oven. Place on a wire rack for 15 minutes to cool. Remove the bars from the baking dish, and drizzle with chocolate topping. Serve.

99. Protein donuts

Ingredients:

- 85 g coconut flour.
- 110 g vanilla flavored germinated brown rice protein powder.
- 25 g almond flour.
- 50 g maple sugar.
- 30 ml melted coconut oil.
- 8 g baking powder.
- 115 ml soy milk.
- 1/2 teaspoon apple cider vinegar.
- 1/2 teaspoon vanilla paste.
- 1/2 teaspoon cinnamon.
- 30ml organic applesauce.
- Additional:
- 30 g powdered coconut sugar.
- 10 g cinnamon.

Directions:

a) In a bowl, combine all the dry Ingredients.

b) In a separate bowl, whisk the milk with applesauce, coconut oil, and cider vinegar.

c) Fold the wet Ingredients into dry and stir until blended thoroughly.

d) Heat oven to 180° C/350° F and grease 10-hole donut pan.

e) Spoon the prepared batter into a greased donut pan.

f) Bake the donuts for 15-20 minutes.

g) While the donuts are still warm, sprinkle with coconut sugar and cinnamon. Serve warm.

100. Honey-sesame tofu

Ingredients:

- 12 ounces extra-firm tofu, drained and patted dry.
- Oil or cooking spray.
- 2 tablespoons reduced-sodium soy sauce or tamari.
- 3 cloves garlic, minced.
- 1 Tablespoon honey.
- 1 Tablespoon grated peeled fresh ginger.
- 1 teaspoon toasted sesame oil.
- 1 pound green beans, trimmed.
- 2 Tablespoon olive oil.
- 1/4 teaspoon red pepper flakes (optional).
- Kosher salt.
- Newly ground black pepper.
- 1 medium scallion, very finely sliced.
- 1/4 teaspoon sesame seeds.

Directions:

a) Set aside for 10 to 30 minutes. Whisk the soy sauce or tamari, garlic, honey, ginger, and sesame oil together in a large bowl; set aside.

b) Cut the tofu into triangles and location in a single layer on one half of the prepared baking sheet. Drizzle with the soy sauce mixture. Bake until golden-brown on the bottom, 12 to 13 minutes.

c) Turn the tofu. Place the green beans in a single layer on the other half of the baking sheet. Drizzle with the olive oil and spray with the red pepper flakes; season with salt and pepper.

d) Return to the oven and bake till the tofu is golden-brown on the 2nd side, 10 to 12 minutes more. Sprinkle with the scallions and sesame seeds and serve right away.

CONCLUSION

There are many things that can help contribute to your success, but the main thing is you! Don't let others get you down, bodybuilding whilst on a vegan diet can often produce negative remarks from others. Chose to ignore it and prove them wrong.

As long as you follow a diet plan that consists of plenty of protein, carbohydrates, fat, fruit and vegetables and progress at a steady rate with the exercises, there is no reason why you should fail. You just need to keep motivated and stick at it. Once you apply all the knowledge and techniques you have learned from this guide, plus your own research, there is nothing stopping you – so get going, and good luck!

www.ingramcontent.com/pod-product-compliance
Lightning Source LLC
Chambersburg PA
CBHW070509120526
44590CB00013B/788